Messages from Heaven

Messages from Heaven

A New Life on Earth

Connie Fox

Copyright © 2016 Connie Fox
All rights reserved.

ISBN-13: 9780692622155
ISBN-10: 0692622152

*Dedicated to
Jesus, Mahavatar Babaji
And the Angels*

I Thank You for this Gift

Acknowledgements

IN GRATITUDE TO my mom, Susan Fox, for her never-ending, unconditional love and support throughout my life. I am truly blessed to have you as my mother and editor.

Contents

	Introduction	xi
Chapter 1	Fullness of Life	1
	Messages 1-9	
Chapter 2	Waking Up	4
	Messages 10-20	
Chapter 3	A Time for Stillness	10
	Messages 21-32	
Chapter 4	A Time for Action	16
	Messages 33-40	
Chapter 5	Open Your Eyes	20
	Messages 41-43	
Chapter 6	The Blossoming of Consciousness	23
	Messages 44-53	
Chapter 7	Stepping Stones	29
	Messages 54-66	
Chapter 8	A New Life on Earth	37
	Messages 67-75	
Chapter 9	Know Your Power	43
	Messages 76-88	
Chapter 10	The Power of God	53
	Messages 89-99	
Chapter 11	A Wave of Darkness	62
	Messages 100-110	

Chapter 12	Soul Awareness ·74	
	Messages 111-120	
Chapter 13	The Second Coming is Through Your Heart · · · · · · · · · · · · · · ·83	
	Messages 121-129	
Chapter 14	New Villages ·93	
	Messages 130-136	
Chapter 15	Falling in Love with Your Life · 100	
	Messages 137-148	
Chapter 16	Stilling the Mind's Thoughts ·115	
	Messages 149-154	
Chapter 17	Lost and Confused · 125	
	Messages 155-158	
Chapter 18	New Patterns · 128	
	Messages 159-168	
Chapter 19	Heaven in Your Heart · 138	
	Messages 169-171	
Chapter 20	Angels Speak ·142	
	Messages 172-182	
Chapter 21	Spiritual Priorities · 166	
	Messages 183-187	
Chapter 22	Your Soul's Call to Awaken ·176	
	Messages 188-190	
Chapter 23	Letting Go · 183	
	Messages 191-195	
Chapter 24	The Collective Shift · 190	
	Messages 196-200	
	In Closing · 193	

Introduction

THE MESSAGES IN this book were given to me between January and September, 2015. I soon came to anticipate these as a focus point for each day. I received one to several messages throughout the day and shared them with others on my blog and Facebook page. They quickly accumulated.

When I sat down to read all the messages in their entirety, I noticed the progressive nature of the conversations and how they reflected and supported our individual and collective consciousness. A new book series was born.

I not only enjoyed these messages, but word for word, I began to feel them in my heart. I think you will too. I know that is the intention with which they were given to us.

Connie Fox
October, 2015

Fullness of Life

Message from Heaven #1

EVERYONE HAS THE ability to experience fullness of life. When you choose to develop it is all up to you. Give your heart and spirit some time and attention. This is all you need to become more aware of your soul's presence and awareness.
Jesus

Message from Heaven #2

Consciousness is a Being. It is one Being. This Being is formless energy. It is what created all there is. This energy is our Father. It is in you, in me and in all. You can become aware of this. You have only forgotten who you are.
Jesus

Message from Heaven #3

I am not an individual being. I am a being who encompasses all within me. You are the same. The only difference between us is that you have forgotten it.
Jesus

Message from Heaven #4

When you start to feel an unease within you, think of me. Tell me about your unease. Share it with me. Put your attention on me. Tell me what you need. Then trust in me to take care of it for you.
Jesus

Message from Heaven #5

Remember your true nature by remembering how you were as a young child; with an open heart not yet filled with pain; a carefree mind and spirit; open to others without judgment; an inner joy for life. Now, feel that. Do this every day for a few moments. Remember who you are. This will awaken your true-self.
Jesus

Message from Heaven #6

There are two parts of you. One is physical and one non-physical. You usually put your physical part first. You put your thoughts, time and energy to this more than to your spiritual self. If you did the opposite, your physical life would be more than you could possibly imagine. Heal your heart and grow your soul. Practice the *HOPE Technique** and the *Heart Technique**
Jesus

Message from Heaven #7

When you are thinking of me, a connection is made to God. You are telling God that you want Him by thinking of me. In time, you will get to know Him – the unmanifest Source of me, you and all. Until then, connect with me.
Jesus

---

* HOPE [Healing Our Past Experiences] Technique©, a tool given from Jesus for effective emotional healing. For more info visit www.DivineUniversity.org

* *Heart Technique*®, a spiritual practice given by Jesus as a shortcut to heart expansion for rapid spiritual growth. For more info visit www.HeartTechnique.com

Message from Heaven #8

I'd like you to understand more about your divine nature; the part of you that is forgotten, although, is as real as it has ever been. It is a difference in awareness of knowing your truth. It is a matter of being more aware of it or less aware of it. Awareness is what brings fullness of life; increased awareness of love.

Your level of awareness is your level of consciousness. You increase it by expanding it. When you understand this, you intentionally seek it. Now life begins to change. God begins to take over your life. Divine life begins to be experienced. This is what you are seeking; living through the unlimited divine nature of yourself which you have lost touch with.
Jesus

Message from Heaven #9

A world exists in your mind. You can make it a good world or a bad world. It all depends on the quality of your thoughts. Your mind's thoughts turn into the creation of your physical life. Your physical world is different from the existence of every other's being. Each and every one of you creates your own world, your own experience by the thoughts you believe in. If you believe in good thoughts, you have a good life. If you believe in bad thoughts, you have a bad life. If you believe in some of each, you have a life of good experiences and bad experiences. You can release your belief in all bad thoughts and experience only good experiences. You are the creators of your mind's thoughts.
Archangel Gabriel

Waking Up

Message from Heaven #10

WHAT IS PRIDE? It is ignorance. If you have it, you are stuck in a rut. The only way out of it is to love a being who you presently do not feel love toward - a plant, an animal, the earth, a person, a fish. The form of being does not matter. You can experience love equally to all forms of beings.

Choose one form of being today that you do not feel much love toward. Now, put some time and energy into loving this being on a daily basis. Give this being ten minutes of your love while alone every day. You do not even have to be with this being. Just send him/her/it your love energy. You will begin to experience an awakening in your heart that had been sealed shut. The manifestations of this action will bring you a new life filled with more self-love.
Archangel Metatron

Message from Heaven #11

Pay attention to your thoughts. Check in with your mind's thoughts frequently. What have you been thinking the last few minutes? Know where your attention goes. It is like a radio frequency. Your thoughts emanate an energy vibration throughout your being. The quality of your energy vibration attracts people and circumstances like a magnet, always with that which is in alignment with the quality of your inner energy. Your inner energy creates every tiny detail of your life. This happens unconsciously. You create your own existence.
Jesus

Message from Heaven #12

Love is the answer to all your problems. But, when your mind's thoughts are not loving thoughts, then you cannot bring more loving energy into your being. Try to make it a priority to pay attention to your thoughts. As you become increasingly aware of them, you can intentionally change them to being more in alignment with loving thoughts. Simply, change the thought. Replace a negative thought, a fearful thought, an angry thought, a stressful thought, with a higher quality thought; a more loving, trusting and peaceful thought.

In a short time, you will start to feel differently about it. It is very systematic and automatic. Create a habit of checking in with your thoughts throughout the day and intentionally replace it with a more loving version. This will snowball and gain momentum quickly. This alone will change your life.
Jesus

Message from Heaven #13

All pain experienced in your life needs to be fully experienced. All suppressed pain must be felt fully to be freed from the underlying fear that caused you this pain. Your pain is always the result of a fear you have. And, all fears you have are a direct result of the fear of being separated from our Creator. You can bypass the many superficial fears you have by going deeply into the one and only fear that creates them all - the pain of the perceived separation from God. Feel the pain of your fear of being lost; incomplete, unloved and unloving. Feel the pain of not feeling whole. Ask for Christ consciousness; the consciousness of Christ.
Mahavatar Babaji

Message from Heaven #14

Many are now feeling a sense of urgency for something more. An underlying feeling of something missing is increasing. It is causing more irritation, confusion, disharmony and dissatisfaction. It is a time in your evolution to acknowledge there is more to you than only your physical self and physical life. Your soul is ready to expand and grow. Intentional development of your spirit-self is needed. Emotional healing is needed to accomplish this. Suppressed emotional pain is the only thing that suppresses the growth of your soul. Emotional pain is healed by acknowledging its existence and allowing yourself to feel it fully.

Healing each and every emotional wound from your past lightens your heart, mind and soul. More love, light, peace and inner joy is experienced. To advance to a more balanced state of healing and well-being, you must give yourself a little time daily to get in touch with your heart's sorrows and pain. The longer you ignore what is there, the more uncomfortable you become with it. Grace enters your life when you honor your soul's calling to awaken. You do this by honoring your pain and those underlying fears that cause your pain. The HOPE Technique is a simple and powerful method I created to heal all of your accumulated pain and fears. It brings awareness to what you have been ignoring. Increased awareness of your spirit-self occurs as you heal your pain and fear.
Jesus

Message from Heaven #15
Love blossoms within you like a flower when you are happy from the inside. Everything in your life becomes infused with the fragrance of love. Your experience of life becomes more than anyone could ever imagine. Loving others without wanting or getting something in return is the way to induce the blossoming of your heart. Loving God before you know Him is not easy. So, give others more love, joy and comfort in their lives because producing this energy awakens your awareness of God. This is how to induce God-consciousness.
Mahatma Gandhi

Message from Heaven #16
Nature is a source of energy with which you can unify. It is a direct channel to the love and peace of God. Being in nature has an extremely powerful

effect on your energy. It is like a baby being enfolded in a soft, warm blanket. Your being will just sink into it the more you are in nature. Your consciousness will easily become one with its peace and life. Time spent in nature supports the expansion of your life energy. All life on earth affects all other life. Nature is your best friend.
Jesus

Message from Heaven #17
Begin changing your life by devoting some time to your spirit-self. If you devote 90% of your time and attention to your physical life and 10% to your spirit-self, your life will be 90% limited; a slow process it will be to achieve fullness of life. It is time to live fullness of life. Most of your lives need to change dramatically to accomplish this. Your goals need to change. How you spend your time needs to change. What you think of needs to change. What you are wanting needs to change. Change your priorities.

Want God and nothing else. Let Him create your life for you. It will be so much more than you could ever begin to desire. You do not know the love and power and joy of our Father. Create a more balanced life and your efforts will be needed no more. Work no more than six hours a day, six days a week. Change your work to something you love doing. Live a simpler life if needed to experience this. Still your mind in a spiritual practice daily. Find your inner calm. Heal your heart. Give without underlying expectations. Be in nature daily. Take care of your bodies. Share your love.
Jesus

Message from Heaven #18
Now is an opportunity to change the world. A breaking point is near with earth's ability to withstand more friction energy. There is now more support than ever to change life on earth. Developing self-sustaining, love-based, intentional communities [neighborhoods or small villages – to be discussed later] are absolutely necessary to accomplish this. You can no longer remain dependent on organizations, businesses and governments for your life and

well-being. You must also grow spiritually. Gather names of people who may be interested in coming together for this purpose. Invite them to unite together. Bring all resources together and create a loving, harmonious community that can live free from forced dependency.
Jesus

Message from Heaven #19

Are you ready to take a stance for Love? Are you ready to grow in harmony toward your true nature? A wave of forgiveness is coming to you all from our Father. It will set all of you free from your self-created disharmony. Some will be staying on earth, some will not. Either way you'll be free to grow again. You've been stuck, stagnant for so long. It is a blessing to be forced to grow. I want to explain exactly what I mean.

It is time to grow. What forces growth? Pain and suffering. I do not want you to experience more pain and suffering. But, if you will not let go of your illusions, a painful route is your only remaining choice. Growth will get you over the fence of suffering, stagnancy, emptiness, sorrow, hostility, anger, resentment, pity, sadness, grief, jealousy, selfishness, self-centeredness and shame. The people who stay here on earth will be capable of growing. It requires only the willingness to grow beyond ego.
Jesus

Message from Heaven #20

When I was on earth, I wanted to give you the understanding, the awareness, that all your suffering is self-chosen. And, that you can turn the cycle around. Some thought I was crazy to announce that loving one's enemy is the way to peace, harmony and fullness of life. It was ludicrous thinking to some. I gave my life to our Father so you could have more time to accept my teachings. Now it is many years later and you still have not grown well. Your wars are bigger and 'better'. The earth is severely damaged as well as your health. Your DNA is no longer fully human due to genetic modifications – combining of two different species into your foods and injected into your bodies. You've disrupted God's grace. All of your pain is His. You are trying to destroy your own Maker.

I cannot stress enough the rare time this is. You must come together with the intention of living independently and growing spiritually. Instead of wanting more things, more positions, more money, more fame, more of everything, become independent in a community and spend time daily learning about loving. It is your spirit-self that is the same as your love. Become acquainted with it. Want that instead.
Jesus

A Time for Stillness

Message from Heaven #21

BEING STILL HAS been talked about in the Bible, but many people seldom practice stillness. They would rather talk about what they think they know. Stop talking about the Bible and practice it through stillness. The Bible has gotten you little grace; very little compared to what is available to you through stillness.

"Be still and know I am God" means to be still. Still your minds. Still your activity. Still your breathing. Still your being. I am found in the stillness; beyond thought, beyond activity, beyond words, beyond the body. I come to all who seek me in stillness.
Jesus

Message from Heaven #22

Make amends to those you have hurt. You know who they are. Think about it, write down their names and send them your love. Send them your love for ten minutes a day for a month. Then consider yourself freed; freed from the pain continuing. Who is to blame or who is right makes absolutely no difference. Send them your love. Free yourself from your own agony.
Jesus

Message from Heaven #23

Come to a new place with our Creator. Your relationship with your Creator can be renewed, restored and realized. Many of you do not know our Father.

You only know what you've been taught. Think for yourselves. Feel your own heart. Instead of being a follower, become a leader to Christ consciousness. Lead yourself to Christ consciousness by surrendering your life to God. You will lose nothing and gain everything. You've been taught that letting go is losing, but it is the extreme opposite.

I demonstrated surrender and service, love and honor to each other. I never demonstrated an exception. Giving to God is giving to others. They are one and the same. If you knew my face was behind your fellow man, how would you treat them? Create unity with God by uniting with all. Your separate groups and organizations and religions create division. Need not to define me. You'll never find me through words or beliefs. Grow beyond beliefs. Get to the heart. It does not divide.
Jesus

Message from Heaven #24

Come to me in a way you know not. This is what you've been missing. You're stuck in your minds where you cannot find me. Come to me through the heart. This means through loving each other. Stop all words. Stop all judgments. Stop your judgmental thoughts. You know the difference between judging and separating versus discernment with unity thinking. Separating yourself from others is what continues your separation from God. Be not a "this" or a "that". Find no fault in the other. Get beyond judging and fault finding. This means going beyond the mind. Just be loving.
Jesus

Message from Heaven #25

Become aware of awareness; the presence behind your awareness. It is a stillness; a being that knows all. Our Father is this Presence. He is a formless Presence. He is the Creative Intelligence *before* the manifestation of form. If God were an individual being, how could you be? He is in you, through you and with you now. It is only awareness that you need. You increase your awareness by giving it your attention. Tune out the noise in your head and

simply put your attention on it. Do this many times throughout the day. Become watchful for this Presence. Remember this Presence is always there. Tune into It.
Jesus

Message from Heaven #26

Where do you go to develop these communities? There is a time coming when all locations south will not be habitable. There will be poisons in the air that cause bacterial infections in the air, water and soil. It will take time for these areas to clean the debris. Places with temperatures about 70° Fahrenheit and below are the best places to be for a while. It is such a pity to have this beautiful land become a disaster. But, the earth will heal. Know this. But also know these locations will need to be uninhabited for a time.

I want you to understand what brings this disaster and sickness worldwide. It is selfishness and self-centeredness. It is all a matter of heart; the quality of your heart. Your minds control your life, not your heart. That is what you've created. Practical advice is now needed. Many of you will read my messages and heed my advice. Many will never read them. Some will simply ignore them. Some will waver between feeling a rightness with my words, but will not feel like inconveniencing themselves to follow them. It is a matter of pride over heart and wisdom. It is your free will to awaken. I am giving you the knowledge you need to awaken here on earth.
Jesus

Message from Heaven #27

A Recommended Prayer from Jesus: *"I am here to ask You, my Creator for a deeper and stronger connection to the Love that You are. I am ready to add more of Your awareness into my conscious awareness. I feel incomplete without You. I feel an emptiness without You. I feel fear without You. My world is a limited world without awareness of You. The less love in my heart, the less aware I am of You. Living life without full awareness of You brings painful* experiences. The pain is there to get my attention and let me know something is missing and incomplete. I have lost the understanding of why we experience pain. The entire world has forgotten this."

"I want You back in my conscious awareness and direct experience in life. Nothing can fulfill me as You can. I want You back. Please show me how I can live a life more in accordance with unifying as one heart, one mind and one soul again. I am lost without You Father. I love You and want to grow closer to You."

Message from Heaven #28

Where is your heart right now? Think about it for a minute. What are you striving for today? What are your goals for the day? What is your main purpose for this very day? Is it for you or for me? Is your intention to please yourself or me?

I am not your commander. I am your life giver. I give more life to those that give me theirs. The result of this is always experiencing more love, peace and joy than your minds could ever begin to conceive. Trust that. Know that. Honor that. Arise each day with the intention to please me today. I do not want you to be a doormat. I want you to experience all that you are but have temporarily forgotten.
Jesus

Message from Heaven #29

I come to everyone who asks for me and lives for me. What you say you are or not, who you think you are or not, what you've done or not, makes no difference. It is the belief in your dreams that becomes your reality. There is another reality above and beyond yours that you can never alter. It is always the same. Your dream world affects it not. This reality is my reality. It is the one and only reality. It contains no fear, only unconditional love. You can experience my reality while still in your body. That's why you are here; to experience life from a place of unconditional love. The only thing you need to remember is to give love around you. This means action. Give love means

to act in accordance with love. Be kind and caring, forgiving and helping. This is all you need to get what you'll receive.
Jesus

Message from Heaven #30
Before you try to change another's belief system, try to understand that all of your belief systems are honored by me. Your beliefs will never be the same as another's. There will always be differences among each other. This is the beauty of life. Your differences make each of you the individuals you are. God did not make you as robots. You are free to express your own reality. There will never be the exact same realities for anyone. This is the beauty of love.

When you want someone to think as you do, believe as you do and be like you, you are missing self-acceptance. You do not accept yourself or love yourself. You want others to be like you for the comfort it brings to your separation-based ego. Know that I made you to be different; each and every one. Trying to go against God's world is fruitless and it brings pain, loss, emptiness, grief and sorrow. Judge not another. Do not ask your brother to think like you, believe like you or to be like you. Love is neither conditional nor judgmental. Self-righteousness is the most self-damaging quality. Be not God, until you are real for Him.
Jesus

Message from Heaven #31
I am coming back again within you. There is no need to create myself again. Your goal has been accomplished. You've been given the light you need to be free. I created that for you when I was on earth. All you have to do is accept me. This means not my body, nor my face, nor a group of beliefs in my name. This means my heart, my mind, my spirit, my consciousness. Develop Christ consciousness within you; in your heart, your mind, your conscious awareness. Cultivate your love. This means give it. Would you rather argue about beliefs or judge everyone? You reject me with these

missed opportunities. You have what you need, but you choose it not when you deny me in this way.
Jesus

Message from Heaven # 32

Give me yourself through your heart, not your mind's beliefs. Your attitude is formed by your heart and your heart is formed by your attitude. Pay close attention to your feelings. How is your heart feeling? Is it open to all? Is it open with me? Being with me means your heart is open. Limit not to whom you open your heart. You will never be with me fully until your heart is consistently open and free. Serve me by serving love. Judge not who deserves it. There is no such thing. That is separation, not unity thinking. That is being stuck in illusion. I am never found nor felt nor seen in illusion. Come together without beliefs. Leave them at the door. Let your hearts take over. You find God awareness through a pure heart; free from all judgment and fear.
Jesus

A Time for Action

Message from Heaven #33

WHAT ARE YOU waiting for? This very moment you could surrender your fear and be with me fully. Making amends to yourself is the very last thing you need to become free. What you convey to your brother, what you place on the other, what you see in another is your perception of yourself. If you could get out of blame and shame, you would be in unity consciousness. You would understand we are all one and undivided. You would be singing for life; for the love for life; the extreme joy within that cannot be understood from words is your true experience. Every day of your life without this experience is a pity and waste of life.

Forgive yourselves, my children. Forgive each other. Stay stuck in blame and shame no longer. Pray every day and give it to me intentionally. Ask me to free you from it. Then give your forgiveness to another through acts of loving-kindness. Do something kind for another each day. This is putting action behind your prayer to me. Your prayer must be made real through your actions. Then leave the rest to me. I will set you free. Remember that you unknowingly created it, so you cannot free yourself of it without my help. Simply give it to me and love another in your daily activity. This is all you need to become fully free.
Jesus

Message from Heaven #34

Being with God requires action; desire and action for God. Do not talk about God for a while until you've begun to understand Him. Instead, perform action for God. Initially, keep your words not expressed about how to be with God. This keeps you stuck in separation from God. Remember that your words come from your mind, not your heart. You need to develop your heart. Until you have this better understood, stay away from words about God. You try to define the indefinable and get stuck in limitation. Focus on the heart; your feelings. Express your love-based feelings in action. Then love blossoms within you. It expands and grows. Then talk about this experience.

It is so natural and easy to unite with God as one. Get out of your minds and words and start doing something. Something that is loving. In a short time, you'll start receiving the love for life, the love for God that you need to truly unite.
Jesus

Message from Heaven #35
When you are confused about me or God or life, be aware of it. This is a good place to be. Following confusion comes acceptance of me to a higher degree. It is when you are certain of the path to God's grace that you are most without it. You will go through a time of confusion about me and God and life. This is a time to rejoice. For your condemnation has dissolved. God has no condemnation. You cannot have both condemnation and God. They are opposing forces.

Acceptance of confusion opens you to God's grace. Then He will take over your life. Reaching a place of knowing that you do not have all the answers is the best place to be. Then your mind becomes receptive to expanding. Your mind does not remain in a box if it is expanding. You will allow higher knowledge to come in when you realize there is more to be known. Being open and neutral minded is a better place to be. God will enter your heart in the most unexpected way. You need to overcome your present beliefs, whatever they are, I assure you. Be open-minded and receptive to new knowledge.
Jesus

Message from Heaven #36
I want to explain divine grace for you. But, know that however I word it for you will not suffice. Knowing God is a direct experience. Words can never

define it. Grace comes into your life when you are giving grace to others. You receive what you give. Grace is a healing, loving, peaceful and powerful energy that infuses into your being. In time they become one. Challenges in life, whatever the form, come from a lack of grace. Your lives can be fully graceful and peaceful and joyful. Give grace.
Jesus

Message from Heaven #37
Many of you are seeking God's grace and try to do well, but are missing the whole purpose. If it is because of fear rather than genuine devotion, grace is not bestowed upon you. It is a chore instead of a heart filled with joy. The difference is what you are cultivating. You've forgotten God, so you must cultivate Him. If you are trying to prevent a judging God or an angry God from finding your faults, you stay guilty in error. Being with God is expressing His love and joy. Cultivate this, not fear.
Jesus

Message from Heaven #38
Can you realize that enlightenment is available to you all? Know that if you cannot believe this is a possibility, it will not be. If you block something in your mind, you cannot create it for you will not accept it. Have a mind that is accepting. I taught you to accept the divine.

There are many experiencing pain and suffering. If you gave it to me and consciously could want no more, your life would be easy and flowing. Think differently if you are in suffering. Think like me, literally. This changes everything and then you will let me in. Judgment is the only thing that causes suffering. Fear is the culprit in the form you are judging. Who or what are you judging? Get to the heart of it. This means feel your fear. Set yourself free from suffering and practice the *HOPE Technique*.
Jesus

Message from Heaven #39

Get to your source of love in activity. Are you spending time doing what you love? A change of pace is needed if you do not have the time to do what you love doing. You need to be more loving so spend your time loving. This includes what you do. So much time is wasted in misery and not enjoying your time. Turn this around. Change your destiny. Enjoy.
Jesus

Message from Heaven #40

Responsibility accompanies growth. When you grow spiritually, your responsibility to help others heal their pain is absolutely necessary. If you do not spontaneously develop the natural desire to help others heal and grow spiritually, your mistaken growth is but a delusion and will become a painful rude awakening.

Growing spiritually begins to develop a natural yearning to share your increased love and joy for life with others. If this sounds like a chore to you, know that you have not begun to develop this yet. Do not judge yourself for this. Simply know it. You cannot feel this if this has not yet been realized. Feel guilt not. But, I want you to understand that when you grow spiritually, an automatic desire to help others grow spiritually occurs. This will become your passion. And it will fulfill you more than any achieved goal of your own.

You can induce the development of this natural process by helping others heal their pain and grow their soul now, rather than later. It may not seem very self-pleasing at first, if you are still living only for yourself. Put the cart before the horse. Induce this expansion of awe and gratitude for life and God, of which you do not yet know.
Jesus

Open Your Eyes

Message from Heaven #41

OPEN YOUR EYES. See what you ignore. Notice how you have become numb like a zombie. You bypass many opportunities to help your fellow man, your devoted animal friends, the plant life which gives life to you; the living water that nourishes you and keeps you alive. My heart is breaking. You have forgotten me. See what I see; the ability to change everything; all misery. Are your things more important than me? I will bring you more than you can conceive. Trust me. Every hurting soul you ignore is a betrayal to me. It directly hurts me. You are turning your back on me. Give me, the Supplier of all, your sincere care. Never ignore a hurting soul. We are one. Do this, not just read it. You know not what you are facing when you ignore the suffering of others.
Jesus

Message from Heaven #42

We used to be in unity. Singing your joy for life was your way of communicating to me. You did this naturally. Joy for life has been suppressed by your unhealed pain and fear. You have so many lifetimes of unhealed pain and fear blocking your realization of me. A time has come that will force you out of your ignorance. You need this help. You cannot feel this love for life without letting go of your pain and fear. So, it becomes God's will against yours until you let it go. Surrender it now, today. You do not have to wait. Change your life. Change your daily goals. I have already given you the answer in such a simple way. Do the *HOPE Technique* and *Heart Technique*

daily. You cannot help but grow quickly if you do this. Expand even more and say my recommended prayer daily (#27). Help someone else be happier today. Save a life. Give your love. Stop and listen to your heart for a minute.
Jesus

Message from Heaven #43

A new day it is. With each new day there is a new opportunity to change your life more toward me. I will explain the unexplainable.

Bliss consciousness is your true state of awareness. It is extreme joy that makes your heart sing. It is divine. It includes no suffering; a life of deep meaning; fulfillment fully realized. God will create this life for you if you allow Him to; if you want Him to.

Try a little experiment. Live for God instead of yourself. Make God your commitment. Implement each practice into your life. Go at your own pace, you choose how long you want to do this. If you find that you do not prefer this way of living, then drop it all.

1.) Pray twelve times during the day, from morning through bedtime. Spend five minutes (or more) talking to me as if I were a close, loving and caring friend. Tell me how you feel. Tell me what you think you need. Pray for at least one other. Now, tell our Father my recommended prayer (#27).
2.) Practice the *Heart Technique* daily.
3.) Schedule some time each day to do the *HOPE Technique*.
4.) At the end of your *HOPE Technique* practice, spend a moment breathing in deeply and slowly, while sitting or lying down. Put your attention on your breath while you are doing this. When doing this, simply know that your breath is life energy that heals your body.
5.) Decide on a way to give one hour (or more) a week of your time to service. Service to humanity, animals or the earth. Make this time of service to someone you do not as yet know personally. Add this time to your weekly schedule.

6.) Write a list of things you love doing. Spend at least a total of one hour a week doing one (or more) of these things. This could be in 15 minute increments four times a week or one hour once a week, your choice.

7.) Create a more balanced life. Simplify your life as needed. Prioritize your life to include these daily practices if you feel you are not able to.

8.) Spend time in nature daily. If you do not have the ability to spend time in nature, then change your life so you can. Ignoring this suggestion will greatly diminish the quality of your life. Make this a priority.

9.) At least once a day before sleep, thank our Father for what you are thankful for.

10.) Throughout the day, pay attention to your negative thoughts. When you notice you are thinking negative thoughts, intentionally change the negative thought to a more loving, trusting and peaceful thought. Do not get caught up in perfection. Just do your best.

11.) Make a conviction in your mind and heart that you are going to give this new way of living an honest and sincere try for your committed time. Tell me once a day that you'd like my help to have the willingness to follow through with doing this. Your ego will create clever reasons why you cannot do this. Just be mindful of this. Reclaim your commitment once a day.

12.) Thank me each day for giving you this knowledge and remember, at least briefly, that I love you beyond measure.
Jesus

The Blossoming of Consciousness

Message from Heaven #44

A MORE BEAUTIFUL world is coming. This is destiny. Get ready for blossoming. Prepare to raise the quality of your inner energy. It's time to refine your energy being. The collective consciousness is already expanding. At the same time, many people's energy is becoming more gross, dense and heavy. This is creating more powerful friction energy. These forces are battling each other at this time. This makes you feel scattered.

It's important during this special time to come together in groups and communities and to blend together your calming and loving energy. When you do this you bring balance to gaps of dark energies. It produces light; loving, calming and harmonious light. It dissolves away these gaps of darkness. Light brings life. I would like many groups and communities to become a reality. This is your strongest force for the collective consciousness.
Jesus

Message from Heaven #45

I am a powerful force and I am your savior. Being able to be "saved" by me means you develop Christ consciousness. It is my heart, my mind and my spirit that must be developed within you. This is my return. It comes from within you. I will give you the specific steps required to know me and unify with me in your direct experience, not only through your mind's limited way of knowing me from beliefs.

1. You first realize that nothing and no one in this physical world can or will fulfill you. Know that to become fully whole in your awareness requires unity consciousness.
2. You heal away the only thing that blocks you from feeling and experiencing me fully, which is your true inherent state of consciousness; pure peace, pure love and pure bliss. This is already within you. It is always within you. The presence of this energy – peace, love and bliss, is our Father's presence. You are here to become one with it; to manifest it fully in your direct experience in physical life. You must face, feel and heal all of your pain and fear. The *HOPE Technique* specializes in mastering this quickly.
3. You intentionally grow your soul. This means to practice a daily program that effectively stills your mind's thoughts and increases awareness of your soul's awareness, wisdom and presence. Practicing the *Heart Technique* develops this quickly and effectively.
4. You must want God. You must want Him more than anything in the physical world. You need to cultivate your love and devotion to Him. I am the connector to God consciousness. Come to me first and I will guide you to Him.

    All of you are my children. Do not separate yourself from me due to your beliefs. Maintain your beliefs as you would like, but develop a personal relationship with me through prayer. This means talk to me as you would a close, loving and caring friend. Do not memorize prayers and repeat them to me to commune with me. Your heart's love does not merge with me as well with rudimentary prayers. Talk to me frequently every day like this:

    a.) Tell me how you are feeling right now. Tell me what's on your mind.
    b.) Tell me what you need help with today.
    c.) Ask me to take care of every task, issue, problem, desire and need. Know that I will do a better job at handling it than you can. Do your best to trust that if you give it to me, I am handling it for you. Your trust in me will grow in time.

    d.) Thank me daily for what you are thankful for.

    e.) Ask me daily that you want to become more aware of what my desires for you are today and that you want to honor that above your desires. Know that my desire for you is a higher experience, a higher love and a higher joy for you than yours are.

    f.) Tell our Father that you want to know Him and that you are my devotee and that you appreciate that He created me for you. You can appreciate me in this way regardless of your beliefs, religion or faith. But, know that as long as you have a belief system that separates you from others, you will not unify with our Creator. Try not to care so much about your beliefs and focus on loving each other instead, regardless of each other's beliefs.

5. Give what you want to receive. Giving what you want will bring more of it to you. Give your compassion, care, help and support to the sick and suffering. You will never reach God consciousness fully until every being in your world is not suffering. You are individual beings within one being that encompasses all. When all beings are healed and free, you will be fully complete. Feeling more and more complete comes quickly when you are actively living your life for God. This means serving and helping His creations; your brothers and sisters, the animal kingdom and earth.

Jesus

Message from Heaven #46
Begin experiencing fullness of life by intentionally healing your heart and expanding your soul. Practice the *HOPE Technique* and *Heart Technique*.
Jesus

Message from Heaven #47
A day comes when there is a calling for your soul to awaken. God's presence wants to be experienced fully through each of you. Letting go and

letting God is a term that has lost its meaning. It simply means learning how to surrender your life to God and accept what God has to offer you. Many think this means to sacrifice some joy for life. It is the extreme opposite. Be more present and connect with your Source; the Source of all.
Jesus

Message from Heaven #48
Before enlightenment, inner growth begins to soar. All of your fear comes to the surface for healing. This brings pain, loss and challenges. An effective way is needed to heal with more ease and grace. For this, I created the *HOPE Technique*. This tool will teach you how to experience painful feelings with acceptance.
Jesus

Message from Heaven #49
When God is experienced directly, the qualities from unconditional love expand. Before you can connect with God's love on a personal level, facilitating this expansion is needed. A daily spiritual practice will assist you with this. The *Heart Technique* is a tool for spiritual growth. Practicing it will begin to connect your spirit with awareness of itself. It begins to infuse within your consciousness. Conscious awareness of your true-self quickly develops. Trials and tribulations dissolve away.
Jesus

Message from Heaven #50
Before your soul can merge with its Source in your awareness, all pain and fear must be healed. Facing and feeling your pain and fear is required. It can be experienced with grace. Acceptance of its existence is achievable with the desire to grow. Until you accept the willingness to grow, the peace of

God is intangible. You will eventually accept its existence. When you accept it is up to you.
Jesus

Message from Heaven #51
Come together in groups and communities for the purpose of expanding your love. Two lights together are brighter than one. Creating a collective consciousness of peace and love must become a priority. You need each other to create a more peaceful inner experience and outer world. Now is the time to come together for this purpose, not a time for living solo.
Jesus

Message from Heaven #52
When your heart is healing and your soul is growing, the love, peace and power of God enters your direct experience. Fear fades away. Judgmental thinking becomes a thing of the past. Disharmony within is no more. This is when you begin making an extraordinary difference in the world. Your light brings life to others and fulfills you more and more. A oneness consciousness begins to re-define you.
Jesus

Message from Heaven #53
Fullness of life is awe for life. Singing from the heart becomes your every moment experience. This is your natural state. It has been lost. Fear predominates. Dysfunction is growing rampantly. Hell on earth is becoming more extreme. You are capable of destroying yourselves. You are the creators of your world. You can change the trend you are on if you come together with the desire to induce spiritual awakening.

You need to bypass your false need for separating religions. As long as there are separating religions, there will be a separating consciousness and unity consciousness cannot be. I brought myself to you in human form to teach you that separating yourself from others is separating yourself from God. You have gained little by my example of loving all regardless of your differences. You were born to be different. You are fighting God's creation if you are wishing others to have your beliefs. This will only bring you pain and emptiness, sorrow and grief. Why do you want to be above others? God is the Creator of us all.
Jesus

Stepping Stones

Message from Heaven #54

HAPPINESS COMES EASILY when your soul is growing.
Jesus

Message from Heaven #55

The heart and soul are one and the same; life, love, peace, bliss energy. This energy flows through the heart and soul. Soul growth is essential for increased love. Healing the heart is essential to maintain life.
Jesus

Message from Heaven #56

When you live for God your whole world changes. Self-forgiveness deepens. Love for others grows like wildflowers. Happiness is sustainable. Worry dissolves. Sickness is healed. You need for nothing. How does one live for God? You surrender your judgments and fears. Instead of living to avoid them, increase your awareness of them and heal them. Then, living for God happens automatically.
Jesus

Message from Heaven #57
Being in love with life is fullness of life. This can be your reality. It is how God created existence. Your accumulation of fear dissolved it away. So, do away with your fear. Feel it and heal it. It is that simple.
Jesus

Message from Heaven #58
When you are too busy for too long, depression develops. It is an unnatural experience. The depression is letting you know something needs attention. Facing and feeling all of your pain is what will set you free. Do the *HOPE Technique* daily.
Jesus

Message from Heaven #59
When you retire at night, think of me.
Jesus

Message from Heaven #60
Many people are wondering if another man of God is coming to earth to lead you to God and change your world for you. This would mean that you are not Sons of God and are unable to reach God yourself. When I was on earth, I wanted you to know that you are all Sons and Daughters of God as much as I am. But, when you are not thinking like a child of God nor talking like a child of God nor behaving like a child of God, you cannot believe this and you cannot know this. Finding God in your direct experience is extremely simple. The challenging part is learning to want to develop God's qualities.

If developing God's qualities sounds like an arduous, boring task that includes sacrificing your joy, you have learned incorrectly. Your concept of God is distorted. God is not angry. God is not judgmental. God is not disappointed in you. God loves you individually and wholly. He wants to merge with you fully. He wants to express His love through you fully. Instead of feeling that God is a task master, know that the more awareness of God you develop within your consciousness, the more joy you feel.

The joy of God expansion within you is what you are all seeking. But until you know Him, you seek this joy, this fulfillment from the outer world – from people, from things and from external situations. Nothing in the physical world will satisfy you nor fulfill you. Coming to this realization is usually very painful. You want your world to be how you think it should be. I'd like to help you understand this more intellectually before you come to know this as truth.

If you turned your thinking around voluntarily, not because you have to but because you want to, you would save yourself a painful future. God is experienced as ecstatic joy; love and gratitude that is beyond your comprehension without the experience. The beauty of God's grace is not able to be realized through your mind. God's grace flows through your heart. Heart development is the way to find me and our Father.

You do not know your soul. You fear it because your mind cannot understand it. Cultivate experiencing it. Do not try to understand it. Understanding your soul comes automatically with the expansion of it. What you avoid is what will unite you with it - your pain and fear. Broken hearts do not merge with the Unbroken. Healed hearts do. God cannot heal your heart without you asking Him to. But, do not ask and then avoid feeling your pain. You created it. You must face it to heal it.

Intentional soul growth will save you lifetimes of pain and suffering. There are two channels to God realization: soul growth and heart growth. God energy needs to flow through your heart and soul to be fully God-realized and to experience your truth. I want you to know this. Your willingness for growth is required. Focus your attention on how you can help others feel happier. This is giving our Father's love to others and to Him as well. Giving your love energy is how you give of yourself. Acknowledge that your spirit needs your attention also - not only your body - your spirit. Give it some time to expand daily. Integrate your conscious awareness with it.

Jesus

Message from Heaven #61
Save yourselves for God. Give Him your life. You do this by thinking about pleasing Him. Get over your prideful mentality. Simply put, recognize you are not your Creator.
Archangel Gabriel

Message from Heaven #62
Have awareness of the words you say. Know that each word you say creates something. All words create something in physical manifestation. This is because your words actually have power; the power to create. This act is accomplished spontaneously. You may or may not be aware that your words are a form of energy that extend out into the Source of creation and manifest something in your physical world. This is how God created life. All you need to do to become more powerful at creating what you want, is to say words that match what you want to create. Your habit of saying negative statements is simply a habit. Conscious awareness of your words will begin to heighten the quality of your words and this will change your life in a powerful way.
Jesus

Message from Heaven #63
Can you begin to understand the importance of changing how you think? If you are not fully God-realized, you need to change your thinking. Develop my way of thinking. The ego's life exists from the thoughts you believe in. So, if your thoughts are not in alignment with my thoughts, there is pain and suffering in your present or future.

My thoughts are loving thoughts. I do not think with fear, separation or judgment. If you have fearful, separating or judgmental thoughts, you are creating experiences in your life that will make you feel more fear, separation and judgment. Judgment is guilt. If you do not want to change your thinking, you do not have to. But, you will cause yourself more pain until you do want to. God is love energy. Why would you not want to have more of Him in your thinking?
Jesus

Message from Heaven #64

Forgiveness is known of but not often experienced. Many think giving forgiveness means to give someone your forgiveness. It is the opposite. Give yourself forgiveness first. This is what makes forgiving others effortless. If someone causes you pain in any way, pay attention to it. The "it", not the person. What is the "it"? It is your pain. What pain are you feeling? Name your pain. Give it your attention, your awareness. It will heal away on its own simply through honoring it. It is the resisting of your pain which keeps it a part of you. The longer you resist it, the stronger it becomes and the more pain it creates. Sit down with it – your pain. Acknowledge it, feel it and honor it – fully. This is the easier way to forgiving others. It is the only way to true forgiveness. You are forgiving yourself when you do this.
Jesus

Message from Heaven #65

A carefree heart I want to define for you. Your heart is naturally like this: open to loving all instantaneously simply because you are brothers and sisters. This statement can mean little to some, for even many blood siblings have lost their instinctual loving. There are no hesitations demonstrating your love for each other. It is automatic. There is nothing to hold you back from expressing your love and care to all. You naturally want to help them if they need help. You naturally want to bring them happiness. You naturally want to give them your joy. It delights you to bring others joy more than anything you could want for yourself.

Your heart swells with love and gratitude to our Father when you are able to give love to your fellow brother. There is no such thing as concern for how others perceive you. You fully love and accept yourself with no reservations. You are so grateful to each other for helping you to be who you are. This quality of loving is natural. It is spontaneous. There is no effort involved to be loving, kind and caring to all. Fear does not exist.

You love the same Father for your life, whatever your minds know. You honor and cherish everyone's unique personality and qualities. You all live your lives for God. You would want it no other way because He fulfills you more than life itself. His love for you is felt and known. There is no greater love than His. You want for absolutely nothing. This is a small taste of knowing your true state.

If you do not spend some time each day to feel your pain – the pain that blocks you from this state of awe for life, it will take many lifetimes to break free from the pains that prevent living your life in fullness. Do you want that or not? Make the *HOPE Technique* a common household name. Make it a daily practice to heal away your pain. In a short time you will wish you had done it long ago. It takes only a little practice at first to become comfortable feeling your pain and fear. Quickly, you will look forward to it because you've started to feel the benefits.

Sickness goes away. Painful conditions fade away. Dysfunction fizzles out on its own. Lack becomes no more. Emptiness is replaced with fullness, a fullness no words can describe. You come to realize your home has been within you all along. There is no more searching for anything. The love for God returns. Gratitude swells within you and it is a joy just existing.

As you heal more suppressed pain, your awareness of God grows through your soul and heart, within your consciousness. Your soul becomes who you are. Your body is only a host and you know this. You have the power to create as I do. There will come a time when you will not understand limitation or fear. You all become masters of the divine.
Jesus

Message from Heaven #66
I'd like to discuss something new now. I want you to better understand how you were created. It will expand your consciousness just hearing this. God began to realize Itself. How God began you cannot fully understand until you become one with Him. But I would like you to be more aware of how you began.

You were born in human form for one purpose: to enable God to experience the physical through physical form; to experience His love. God could not contain His love unexpressed any longer. The nature of love is the expansion of it. The force of this energy is absolutely unknowable. Segments of life in physical form burst into physical existence all at once. Human beings came at a later date. With progression and evolution, there came a time when existence on earth was ready for beings with a higher state of consciousness. This means beings with the ability to express God fully.

The first man and woman were born not as babies, but as husband and wife; soulmates; the perfectly loving female and male. And life was good. Humanity began. For a long time, all experienced this way of life. But, with freedom to choose your life comes the opportunity to take over your life; to develop the thought that you are your Creator. With this tiny thought, came a more self-centered way of thinking. Living became more about you and less about loving. Now you are reaching a time of total God denial. Even those who believe in God's existence cannot easily apply God into their daily lives.

Very few on earth have fully surrendered their lives to God. These few souls are feeling God's misery effectively. They are keeping the collective force of your fear from expanding. Now it is a time for you to make a choice; a conscious choice. Do you want to grow spiritually and are you willing to do so?

Earth needs to annihilate those who choose to remain ignorant, thereby contributing more fear. They will inhabit a different more suitable planet which will force them to grow. It is a gift from our Father to help end your pain and suffering. But, this planet is not the lovely and beautiful earth. It would be a pity to need more suffering to break free. Many of you are ready to grow. You are capable of growing. So, you will remain on earth and create harmony again; a new life on earth.

There will be a time of destruction and transition. The people who know they do not intentionally cause harm may feel rejected. However, know that there are no victims. You have ignored the suffering of many. You support the torture of animals. You know people and children are starving, sick and hurting. Earth is suffering from your damage. You choose ignorance over loving and caring and giving. There is always a consequence for every action and every non-action you choose. It is simply cause and effect. There is no judging, merely cause and effect. This is what some call karma.

Your pride has become your 'everything', while you think you are hurting no one. Your perception is a delusion. No one should be suffering. There

is much suffering on earth and your cars and houses and jewelry and things and social status and employment positions are more important. This means more important than me. I am the Creator of your soul. You are destroying your world. You will wake up your dormant hearts one way or the other.
Jesus

A New Life on Earth

Message from Heaven #67

Now, what are you going to choose? What are you going to do? It is all up to you. You have God's support whatever you choose; support toward growth in whatever form you need. God wants you to want Him so you can become free.

So, begin by creating thriving communities that are capable of being free. Rely on each other within the community. But remember to depend on God as the Prime Source and Supplier of all your needs. The governments of the world are going to destroy themselves. You cannot rely on them to lead you in safety and harmony anymore. I will say it again: need no one but your Creator. This is being free.

Now, for how to get this new life on earth started. Make a plan with others who support a loving destiny. Share your thoughts and feelings. Then you need a property. Bring people together who can support one another on your new journey to creating love for life again in peace and harmony and joy to your highest potential.

Make these communities no larger than 300 people. I will tell you why. If they are larger than this, governments will see you as a bigger threat and will tear down your community. They want you dependent on them. They are trying to take God's place. Their perception sees not what I see. Illusion is their reality. Be fully independent in this community. Become able to provide all you need for yourselves.

Meditate together within this community - a certain time in the morning and before dinner. Eat food in its natural state. Pray together. Enjoy life together. Make this property in a nature setting. Utilize nothing that poisons yourselves or the earth. Share what you are learning with each other. Have no secrets amongst each other. Try to be true to one another. Discuss your feelings when negative feelings arise. Support one another through this time of healing and rebuilding. Teach children not to fear God, nor themselves, nor you. Honor their feelings. Create a new generation with much less fear. In one generation our present earth, filled with emptiness and sorrow, pain and despair, wars and famine, sickness and separation, can become a thing of the past.

This is how quickly you can become whole again with me. Fear not the outer world. Focus on your inner world. This is what will help.
Jesus

Message from Heaven #68

Make it a wonderful beginning toward your new life. Make it happy. Rejoice for me. This time and place I have been waiting for so long. You are my children and I love you. I treasure you. You are my world. I need you with me. I want you by my side where you belong. Our Father is waiting for you also. He is in love with you always. Change can come so easily; just be willing. You are on my side for eternity. You can never ever lose me.
I am right here. You have only forgotten me. Feeling me is all you need. Father is waiting so patiently. Give us your heart. Let us fill your heart. Let us guide you back home with us. Give us your life. Let us take care of everything. Just want to do this. I will do the rest.
Jesus

Message from Heaven #69

I am coming back again within you, this I have explained. I want to explain more about my consciousness. Christ is a term that defines me. It means all loving. I want you to clearly understand the qualities that come from me. Love-based qualities are: gratitude, trust, compassion, joy, peace, fullness, patience, understanding, humility, sharing and happiness. These qualities are feelings. You feel more of these the more you love. When you experience these feelings to your highest potential, you are a Christ, like me. This simply means fully loving.

Your minds are able to think how they choose. You have freedom to think any way you'd like. But your minds have great limitation. These feelings I've mentioned cannot be felt with the mind. So, your minds are better left out of this. Use them as you need to live and learn and grow and communicate. But when it comes to developing Christ consciousness, leave your minds out of it. Let your heart be your guide. This means your feelings. Until you know your truth from your own experience, try not to define me.
Jesus

Message from Heaven #70

Surrendering is easy if you trust me. But, what do you do when you don't know me well enough to trust me? This is exactly how you surrender your life to God:

- You think about Him more and more each day. If you are not thinking of Him, your consciousness does not include Him. Think of Him as often as you can throughout the day. These times you are thinking of Him, need nothing from Him. Simply, want to give Him your devotion in this way.
- Thank Him often for what you have. Think not about what you do not have. If you think with gratitude about what you do have, He will give you more and more goodness. Acknowledge Him as your provider for He is the provider of your life and all you have.
- Give Him your grace. This means help His children, His animals and His earth. Ask Him for what you feel you need; every single need. Ask Him to take care of everything. Know He is the Creator of this world, not you. This will help you surrender your resistance to what He wants. In time you will come to know that His way is always your best and highest choice. You will come to know this and trust Him.
- Simply know that He knows better and do not resist Him. This means do not resist what is happening this very moment. Many of you resist

almost everything life brings your way. When you are resisting what is happening, you are resisting God. This is your biggest obstacle. Just give in to His will, accept God's will every moment, every day. This does become automatic in time as you develop your trust in Him.
- Try to be kind, caring and loving to all, including yourself.
- Ask God for help getting to know Him better. This means for you to personally **feel** Him more, not only to understand Him through the intellect. If your feelings for Him are genuine, He will expand from within.

Jesus

Message from Heaven #71

Can you understand the importance, the significance of surrendering your life to God? This is the turning point of all your lifetimes. This is the moment you've been asking for. You may have no idea that every time you ask for something, what you are really seeking is God to take over your life. With the desire to live for God, to serve God, to want Him more in your experience, comes His almighty presence. He comes to those who want Him, who are devoted to Him, who want to join together with Him. If your main goal is to please Him, you begin to become Him, simply because you want Him. He is there and available always. But, you must get to a place of wanting Him. This is usually a very long journey.

I'd like to invite you to induce wanting Him before you may fully understand what this really means. You do not have to wait to get there slowly. Turning your life over to God and asking Him to be your guide is the life-changing moment for you all. It is the moment your soul has been waiting for. You need not know why this is of significance. Just try it for a while.

Jesus

Message from Heaven #72

There is a special way to connect with me. Say these words to our Father: *"You are me and I am You. We are already one. I am not separate from God.*

I only need to remember we are one. When my awareness remembers this, I realize that my God-Self is the one I have been seeking all this time."

"Within my conscious awareness, within my knowing and understanding, I am also all other life. Nothing is separate from me. I am born without this knowledge of truth because I am born into a separate body and world. I need to learn how to let go of how my mind knows, so I can become aware of this awareness. This requires the dying of who I think I am. Surviving is my instinct. But, if I understand this message to a certain degree, I can skip the fight for survival. Acceptance of this will enable everything else that is needed to become one again in my conscious awareness".
Jesus

Message from Heaven #73

Pay attention to these messages, even if you do not believe this is me. Pay close attention. How do you feel? The mind plays tricks, but not the heart. You need no one to tell you who you are. Listen to your feelings. They connect you directly to me. I want you to become more aware of your heart's wisdom and your soul's presence as one.

Can you not look around and see what you have become immune to? There is no guessing the trend you're on. I cannot take away what you all created without your open willingness. You created it, you must want to correct it. Otherwise, you'd just do it again. Believe this is me or not, but open your hearts enough to do something about it. Bring back God's way of living. Now it's time for action. Tonight, before you sleep, kneel on your knees to our Father and tell Him you give Him your life. Surrender yourself fully in the kneeling position. This makes it more real to you. Try to create a community in love's name, not any other.
Jesus

Message from Heaven #74

When all of you are singing your joy every day, you'll look back to this one and feel the most incredible feeling for your life. You'll see how you

brought freedom to all – freedom to live fully. You'll be one with God then and be on no trend. You'll be home inside.
Jesus

Message from Heaven #75

Can you imagine life on earth when everyone lives together as one? Everyone is happy. No one is in stress. There is no such thing as depression and sickness. You sleep like a baby with a smile on your face. You are at total peace. When you reach this place, miracles start to happen in another way. You realize your power. You become masters of your world, not the other way around as a slave in bondage going with the crowd. You become masters of life.

Right now, there is a negative connotation with the word power. Many have destroyed this beautiful, natural process. Where is your power? You all have it the same. You follow behind in your way of slavery. Wake up and get out of it. With my help, you are not helpless. I can only help you grow. If you are on the wrong path, I sit in waiting. I am here to help you come to our Father. Free hearts have my full assistance. You know not what I am capable of. Come to me alone. Tell me you are ready to be free. Follow my other guidance. I will bring you all the assistance you need. You are not waiting for me. I am waiting for you.
Jesus

Know Your Power

Message from Heaven #76

Come to a place of knowing your power. If you had a billion dollars in the bank, but did not know how to write a check, you would not have access to it. This is where many of you are. You have spiritual power. It is a limitless power. There is no end to it.

Whatever you believe becomes your reality. You believe in a power other than Me. Fear is your other power. It is man-made, not God made. It is not even real. But, your physical world is created by you and whatever power you choose.

How do you surrender your fear? You replace it with me – my power, my way of living, my way of loving, my way of giving, my way of thinking, my way of surrendering. You simply give it to God. You cannot do it without His help, so you try to give yourself to Him instead of to your fear. It is that simple. God does the rest.

Transition your thinking toward what you can do for Him rather than what you can do for yourself. It is that easy. Each morning, ask God, *"What can I do for You that I think you would be happy about"*? What comes through your heart? Write it down so you do not forget. Then do it. Begin each day in this way. This will open your heart to Him. When you open your heart to Him, you become an open channel to His power.

Jesus

Message from Heaven #77

Many of you are beginning to wake up and feel more of my calling you to awaken. It is my love you are feeling. It starts with a tiny light within you. It is not even noticed at first, for you are usually too busy to feel it. But, with every kind thought, every loving feeling felt, every action of giving not for self, is what expands this light. A feeling of wanting more of this fulfillment grows. At first, you seek outside of yourself to fill the feeling of something missing. Eventually, you realize nothing in the outer world can fulfill it. This is when you become a seeker of my life.

Then, many get caught up in another way of ignorance; self-righteousness. You unconsciously become a stronger judger and you judge people away. You join groups and religions that strengthen separation. You have good intentions, but gain more ignorance. Some do this in my name, but know it is for your own gain. You need to feel higher and better to cover your discomfort and this will help you feel better for a while. But then, you begin to feel more rejected followed by confusion. Then bitterness becomes your new identity. This is a sad shame. Your bitterness grows and your heart becomes shut. Most die in this way.

You are reborn at the same place to start over again. Usually, this is a several lifetime process of painful, shameful lives. Self-loathing becomes strong. Addictions often follow. This frequently leads to suicidal thinking. Then a rare opportunity arises. Since you are so broken and lost, you finally surrender it all; self-condemnation. In one instant you change your life due to a surrendering. Now you have a spark of life again and you start to grow quickly.

Groups that acknowledge themselves as above, higher or better than others are to be given your close attention. Do not follow them in ignorance. Pay attention to how you feel there. Feel the energy of others with outsiders. How do they feel about them? Do the words, *"if they only knew what we did, they'd be included"* come out of their mouths? If this is their mind set, know this is not a way to bring the world together. Pay attention not to outer appearances in whatever form or belief systems as who you are; pay attention to their hearts. Do they include all or some that are like them? This makes all the difference.

Jesus

Message from Heaven #78

Have a mind, but know how to use it rightly. Your minds have taken over your life and world. Can you understand that what comes from the mind is always a perception? A perception is a way of thinking. Thoughts are not real. You have the gift of thinking, but instead of simply utilizing it, you came to believe you are it. What you think is not who you are. You're completely caught up in a fantasy world. If you could slow your lives down and begin to relax, so many feelings would come up.

At first, it would be many painful feelings in one form or another. But, in a short time, you would come to realize some feelings you do not know. A peace that passes all understanding comes to the surface. It is the most wonderful feeling. Nothing could compare to it. Then beautiful things start happening. The most incredible things you never thought possible. I cannot even put any words to it. Love blossoms within you like a flower. Rays of sunshine come out from inside; an inner joy that is indescribable comes alive. Hearts join together as one – one by one. Then all of a sudden, your heart merges with them all and our Father and ecstasy has returned. Can you imagine living in this state? If you can, then you're using your mind rightly.

Jesus

Message from Heaven #79

A day is coming soon, but before there will be time to prepare for it, it will be gone. These words of wisdom I am speaking to Connie, many will disregard. I want to help you understand how Connie can communicate with me and why it may be hard for some to believe.

All of you, every single one of you were here on earth before. There was a phase in life that you all created, by my so-called religion, where connecting with me was forbidden. Words in the Bible were tainted. People wanted Father's power within them. They wanted it for themselves and not others. They created a new sickness of extreme doubt of what came naturally with your increased loving for me; gifts, what you call special gifts, ways of communicating to me and our Father; ways of hearing me directly. You started to realize your power. Since their hearts were in the wrong place with me, they became jealous. They wanted it only for themselves.

A deeper level of envy was created. So, they decided to take away your power. Their pride grew stronger as did their envy toward me and in time they decided to completely reject me. They created rules to keep you away from loving me. They brought tears and bloodshed and much suffering. They stole your babies. They forced you into submission without me. They created a name for the new god on earth and that became a new world religion by which to live. In time, you all forgot your gifts. You pushed them far away. Now you feared them. This phase lasted a long time and you completely lost them.

There is a deep level of fear associated with them now. There is something within that is left to be healed; a deep pain from rejecting me. Know that if you had chosen to believe in yourselves and doubt me not, I would have been able to change everything with your help. But, what you choose to believe is your destiny. And, I had to let you carry that out.

Know this: what you want to believe is your truth. It may not be reality, but it is to you. All you need do to change your world or what you believe, is to ask yourself, *"is this belief supporting my love and my power or the fear of a devil"*? How can you tell the difference? If gifts emerge in the world and they seem to bring you closer to me, what is it all about? Does it empower you directly or make you more afraid? Does it make you dependent on another man to go to heaven? Do you feel more shame or liberation? Does your heart yearn for more or does your mind's fear take over? Do you follow your heart or your head?

God is never to be feared. You have learned to fear your own Creator. Now what brings you closer to me, you want to reject. Communicating to me directly is a natural gift; one of many. And many of you simply will not accept this. You are repeating the past all over again, staying in ignorance. Give yourself permission to explore what you've been told is the devil. Pay attention to your heart. Logical thinking alone can set you free from this trap. Why would our Father not want you to know Him directly? He is not meant to stay at a far distance. You are here to remember Him. How can you remember Him if you fear letting Him in?

If you witness a way of connecting with me, know that it is to be an inspiration to open up and grow more. It is not only for the other. You all have these natural born powers. Do not fear the word power because the jealous turned this word into something evil. You have all the power I do, not any less. Expand your thinking.
Jesus

Message from Heaven #80
I was not just a human and neither are you. What is within us all is all powerful. It is not human. Why do you not want to investigate this further? What makes you avoid your soul? Your spirit-self is your permanent self. Why do you fear it? Give your thoughts an examination.

What do you think of each day? Where is your mind most of the time? It is not on your spirit-self. You've accepted such a loveless world; a lifeless life. Why? What do you fear? A creator of some kind exists. Don't you want to know it? Think back to an earlier day. Where did you learn God is not within you already? Don't you want to search for Him? Whatever you have your attention upon, grows. Most of you know this, but still live in ignorance. Don't you want to wake up? How long will you accept so little when there is so much to be given? You want more peace, happiness, abundance and fulfillment, yet you fear it. Be with me please. I am longing to be together as one. Go beyond your physical world. Go for it all.
Jesus

Message from Heaven #81
Before you get defensive or angry, think about my words for a minute. What are you really hearing? Some of you will say, *"Thank God I'm not the only one feeling this way"*. Some will feel the opposite. Anger is anger and all anger is fear. There is no such thing in my reality. Wouldn't you prefer my reality?
Jesus

Message from Heaven #82

Have a helping hand today. I'd like to ask you to do something for me. Plan your day to include helping an unknown friend. Help at least one person today; one whom you do not already know.
Jesus

Message from Heaven #83

I am here to help you become whole with me. I can tell you again and again that you are already whole and at one with me. But, if **you** do not know this, it is not your reality. If you choose not to know it, then you will not. You have the freedom to choose your own reality. A new way of thinking is needed to change your present reality. This requires your willingness.

You can read my words again and again, but if you choose not to apply them, you will not gain much from them. What if you made a commitment to your higher-self, just to see where this would lead? Creating a new life on earth requires a new way of living. What if you were to just try it temporarily to see what it creates?

You know not the outcome of every single day, yet you continue to strive for the unknown. Why not become followers of my words for a little while and see what comes of it? If you need more faith in me, just try this and see. Stagnating where you are will not bring you more. Turn your lives around to a higher experience. If you do not prefer it, you can come back again.
Jesus

Message from Heaven #84

It is a wonderful time for incredible growth. A huge transition is coming. This is such a blessing. Stagnation is not being supported anymore. Yes, this is a blessing. I see many communities existing throughout every country. These small spots of expanding love energy are beaming out. This highly loving energy combines in the cosmos where God brings creation to it. It manifests something. What it manifests is increased support toward unity in your mind and heart. You are the creators of your world. What you give out to

it comes back to you in manifest form. It's so easy to create what you want. You just give it. These communities will become your sanctuary. You will be left in peace. I will support this. I anxiously await you seeing what I see. These communities are energy locations that are going to create a new earth.
Jesus

Message from Heaven #85

I will give you more awareness through this message. Before the physical world was created, there was absolutely nothing. In time, this nothingness became aware of itself. Pure awareness was born. Pure awareness is what is in our form. It is pure stillness. Since your bodies live in activity; action, movement, thinking, feeling and sensing everything, this stillness can only be found when you still your bodies, minds and physical sensations. In this pure stillness, is your Life Force. It is your power.

Ever so gradually, you became busier and busier in activity. Your memory of where your power comes from has been forgotten. Now you scurry around each day in a blur. The presence of who you are has been lost in your awareness. This presence is our Father. He is the Life before all form arises. He is what gives life to all form. You know your forms well, but have forgotten where you come from. This is your true self. It is who you are before your human form. Since it is formless, you fear it. It seems like emptiness but in truth, it is fullness. It is fullness beyond your understanding. It is a completeness of everything within it. There is nothing empty about it.

But, your minds cannot understand this no matter how hard they try. And what the mind cannot understand, it fears. When you know only what your mind knows, you live from its level of understanding, which is extremely limited. You must allow yourself to grow beyond your mind's level of experience if you want to be whole - whole minded, whole hearted and whole in your direct experience. But, if you do not know what this means, it does not have much significance to you at this time.

Still, there is something inside each one of you that yearns for something more. Since you only know your outer form and outer world, you think what you need comes from there. Yet, it is another form you keep and it will never make you feel complete. It's a never ending aimless seeking for 'something'. You've been with this lack of consciousness for so long, not knowing you are living in a dream world. You are stuck in your dream world. It is to be enjoyed, that's why you are here. Yet, you've forgotten the Whole that is real.

All you need do to start remembering who you are beyond your form, is to tap into your Source. This is where you find fullness. It is who you really are. You've forgotten your true-self. I've given you the knowledge to find your Source. You will not understand the significance of it until you do find it. So, I invite you again to put your trust in me and follow my guidance. Just give yourself a chance to see what becomes of it.
Jesus

Message from Heaven #86

Many are starting to wake up inside just from reading my words. If you are still reading them, know you are ready for them. This means you are ready for my life. Do not get scared by hearing this, thinking it may mean giving up something you value. Your automatic thought about me is often incorrect. So many have fear or guilt associated with me and my way of living. My life is a life filled with fullness and joy and laughter and love and harmony. Just be open to trusting this please.

My life, my way of living takes away nothing you want and gives you everything you do want, but have forgotten is possible. This being said, acknowledging you are a part of me is needed. Just a tiny thought of this acknowledgment is needed to be accepted. Without your acceptance of me, I cannot force myself to expand within you. You must want me. When I say this, I am referring to my consciousness. This means having the ability to accept my depth of loving.

Acceptance of more love is what this means. Do not make it over-complicated. Do not bring judgments to it. Do not fear what I have to offer. I am not ever going to punish you. Get this thought out of your consciousness please. Your perception of me has been distorted. I am here to bring you back to your true state of loving. There is no sacrifice involved with this. The word sacrifice has been interconnected with me, not by me, but by people in a state of ignorance. Please simply acknowledge this.

Ever since I was born as Jesus, people began to create their own version of me. At that time, the word sacrifice was a strong belief. People believed in animal and human sacrifice, thinking this was in alignment with God. This has left an inner fear within you that needs more awareness to heal.

Simply, recognize it is false, not real. I came to you on earth in human form as your friend, your brother, your Father, your Creator, to bring you the awareness you need to come back to me. Know there is no sacrifice involved with this; not for you and not for any another.
Jesus

Message from Heaven #87

When you have digested my words some more, come back and read them again. You will notice a big difference. Upon reading these words you are absorbing more of my consciousness. It is the most powerful force in existence. You have it also. I'd like to explain more about the power of love and exactly what that means. I want to help you get past the fear of your own power – my power – God's power.

This power is Life Energy and, as I have said, it is formless. There is a miraculous creation that occurs with the combination of your love for me and a simple desire; such a gentle desire, it's more like a little wish without attachment. This is when your power to create gets maximized to infinity. It is that second that occurs just when it enters your consciousness, before you even think about it. This could be called a pure desire.

What this means is that it comes to you spontaneously. In actuality, it's a desire directly from God. It is not a desire that comes from your mind, but from your heart. This makes a big difference in the power behind it. There is absolutely no limitation to it. You are all learning how to tap into God's wishes.

I will offer you a suggestion. If you at least think of God as someone watching you and what you do, not as a stern Father waiting to see something wrong in you, but as a loving Father that always loves you no matter

what you do. And, imagine that you love Him back so much. Now think of how you may want to make Him proud of you for all He has given you and you are so grateful. You'd naturally want to please Him, wouldn't you? If this sounds like a turn off, know that your heart is in the wrong place. Just be open to changing it. If you felt like this toward our Father and simply tried to please Him in all you do, you have no idea what He would bring to you. Just try this pretend game for a little while.
Jesus

Message from Heaven #88

Help a person in need of more happiness today. Find a way today to bring more happiness to another. Make it someone you do not know well.
Jesus

The Power of God

Message from Heaven #89

THERE IS A new born light near awakening within you. It is my love and power. Your acceptance of reading my words has given you more light. Remember when I said it starts with a tiny spark of light and then what you give it, brings more life to it? Expanding your light is the only thing that is needed. This brings more creation to everything else. Stay with me in your awareness throughout your day. Have the intention of expanding your light. Surrender this increased power to me and I will bring what it needs to grow. This will fulfill you with more love and joy.
Jesus

Message from Heaven #90

Many on earth have already begun to shine their light; our Father's life. Emerging from it brings a natural happiness that is not dependent on anything outside of yourself. This may be called a spiritual awakening. It occurs from making that first contact with your higher self. This is a time on earth to awaken your soul self. Many of you are already on your way. This specific message is for them.

Communities need to be created quickly. You are the leaders of my way of living. You understand that acceptance of ignorance is needed, while at the same time trying to help put an end to it. It requires patience; extreme patience. Know that you are not alone on your journey of helping. I am with

each and every one of you personally. In a very short time, you will have increased support; it is near. Remember to ask for my personal help.
Jesus

Message from Heaven #91
Whenever you are feeling fearful about something, or simply worried, follow this advice to put an end to it: engulf yourself in it fully. This is the only way to achieve freedom from it. Your fear will continue again and again, in varying forms, but it is all the same fear. It is the fear of being incomplete, separated from our Father. Your mind wants to attach this fear to something in its world, that is, the physical world. The source of all your fears comes from this one false belief. Get to the core of all your fears, which are behind the stories formed by the mind. Every story is a farce. Don't stay stuck in it. Do the *HOPE Technique*.
Jesus

Message from Heaven #92
Can you begin to understand the significance of this time on earth? It is a time like no other. There is a new earth being formed in the source of creation. What you give it today creates what will manifest tomorrow. At this time, there is no changing the destiny of a needed new planet. Some of you are going there. Some are still on the fence. Others are bringing more love to earth and you are the healers and rebuilders.

All of you create your world each and every day. When you don't consciously feel this from your heart, it seems unimportant. However, know that it is not. I want to get past your unconsciousness with this message and help you wake up. Choosing to go about your day in a self-centered or unconscious way, will become a deep regret. It will become a challenging pain to heal. The power from your heart right now has increased influence in your world. This is because there is increased collective consciousness. There is increased power with stronger feelings. Where there is more fear, there is more love needed to balance it. The earth's collective fear is growing stronger. Right now, I am needed to keep love from being over-powered by fear. You have to learn how to do this for yourselves. I will not support your stagnation much longer.

I want to express the importance of this time, for what has already been created is now unstoppable; a new life on earth and a new planet to inhabit. My heart will break with each one of you who goes to this new planet. It will be a long journey with increased suffering. This will help you let go of your fear. Many of you are able to change the need to go there. Some of you are not. It is already inevitable.

Regardless, the energy you give out, in thought, feeling or action, does make a significant difference in the outcome of your future. If you resist this or feel defensive hearing this, it is because your heart is not in the right place. You create the experiences you receive. You create loving experiences for yourself when you give love to others. When you give the opposite, you bring yourself pain and suffering. This is how life always works. Give of yourself every day in a loving, caring way. You will be grateful for it.
Jesus

Message from Heaven #93

Can you understand more about our Father now? Can you understand that He is not a He? In your English language, God could be called an It. I will continue using your common word of preference, but know God is not a He. God is what was and is, before there was ever a he or she.

When the Bible was written and then rewritten again and again, no one involved in this process could understand a formless God. At that time, men ruled the world and they thought of God as a male; an authoritative, separate and male being. The men who copied the Bible wrote about the god of their understanding. They translated the words according to their level of consciousness; their level of understanding.

Formlessness means no form. Think about this for a minute. This formlessness must be a life force. It brings life to all life forms. So, can you better understand how God experiences Itself through all form? He literally feels what every life form feels. I am the Life Force that is in every cell of your body. This is how I know how many hairs are on your head.

I am your sister, your brother, your mother, your father, your friend, your neighbor, all strangers, every animal. I am the planet earth. I am everywhere. What you give to another, you give directly to Me, your Creator. I do not experience more than a mere fragment of what I am through most of you. You limit Me greatly. You limit yourself. If you surrendered your will, your wants, your desires to Me, I would show you all that is possible.

You're in a catch twenty-two now. You cannot know this until you do. Therefore, you do not want to. So, a leap of faith may be needed to find out. Try applying my simple guidance. My suggestions are extremely simple. I – the Life Energy that I am - will do the rest to wake you up.
Jesus

Message from Heaven #94

Many helpers from other worlds are trying to help humanity and earth. They know how to promote Life Energy in needed areas. They see what is near. They are as loving beings as you are capable of being. They do not have the choices humans have been given. They know no such thing as separation. They are always in harmony with God's love. This message is from their wish to be heard. I will repeat their words:

"We are reaching a time where we can come closer and be seen. We want this so you can hear us. Without our bodies there, you cannot hear us from afar. But, we wait to do this because you are not ready to accept us yet. We could join with you as helpers of your world.

Even though we inhabit at a far distance from earth, we are very affected by you. Your energy carries beyond earth's cosmos and comes to us. It hurts us. It is painful energy. It depletes us. It limits us greatly. We hurt for you, but also for ourselves. We want to help you understand how to bring harmony back to your land. We could be friends; the dearest of friends.

We know how to bring life forms more life. We have more of God's power available simply because we honor Him. We know how to share it well. We live for each other. We cannot imagine living how you live. You don't even know about this. We wish you well and we hope this message sticks with you

and your memory, so when we can meet personally you will be more open to us. Please know we are your friends".
Jesus

Message from Heaven #95

I am within you. Remember this. Bring it fully to your consciousness. With this being on the forefront of your mind, you will automatically find more peace. We are not separate. Just know this in your head for now. If you do nothing else but remind yourself of this, your consciousness will expand and continue to grow. Unity thinking brings unity living and loving.
Jesus

Message from Heaven #96

Whenever you are feeling lonely, think of me and how much I truly love you. When you are feeling lonely, it is because you have lost touch with my love. It is so easy to fill your emptiness with my love. Just think of loving me. To accomplish this, allow yourself time every day to connect with me. What many of you value most are your material accomplishments, not realizing your higher self. What do you give more of your time to? This is what you value most.

Many of you want to turn your lives around to a more fulfilling place, but are caught up in the rat race of your self-chosen life. You may want out of it in your mind set, but you do nothing different about it. Remember that you create your life. Since you do not know how to change your world as it is, or how to get out of its craziness, give your desire for more love and fulfillment to me. This requires connecting with me intentionally. This energy you give to me, I will manifest into what you need. Many of you do not do this and your world grows in more lack of consciousness, more unbalance, more pain and suffering, dysfunction and a sicker world.

Connect with me daily as much as you can. Make this a priority. There is not much time left to turn your lives around in the opposite direction. You must make these changes soon to be among the healers and rebuilders. I will give you specific instructions again for how to become more in alignment with your soul's wishes. Your soul is waiting to be wanted. It is yearning to grow. Give your lives to it, not your houses and cars and clothes or your so called high standard living. This is the first change needed. You will find out that your soul can create more abundance in every way than your minds have ever thought about.

This means giving your energy out for the purpose of healing and rebuilding your lives and your world; your energy in time, in money, in thinking, in feeling, in activity and especially in stillness. What can you do today to help bring a community together? How can you make changes to have more time available to devote to this and to connect with me more? Stillness will not be comfortable until you make progress healing the unexpressed pain and fear within you. Do not forget to do the *HOPE Technique* daily. Expand your soul intentionally with the *Heart Technique*. Remember to help bring more happiness to someone each day. I could go on, but I have explained it already. Go back and read my previous words. You can change the trend you are on.
Jesus

Message from Heaven #97

What do you want? I want to bring the answer to this more in your awareness. Write down a list of all you want. When you are done, come back to reading this. Now look at your list. What does it not include? This is likely what you need to do. You have it backwards. When I say "do", I don't mean you. Leave the doing to me. Still your activity to connecting with me. I will bring life to your goals and dreams.

This requires a letting go of your present way of living. It may seem foreign at first. Most all of you are addicted to action. This is the least effective way to create anything. I am unlimited. Still yourselves and consciously give me your wishes. Spend your time in this stillness and allow me to bring life to it myself. This may make no sense for a little while, but try it and see. Literally, spend more time doing nothing and silently give me your love and devotion. This love you give will blossom and become more and more felt. Then you will come to realize that I am now governing your life. This is when grace enters your experience. Effort is needed less and less. You gain power – my power to create.

Miracles become a daily occurrence. You will start to absolutely love your life. You will want to give me your love more and more. In time you will be laughing and singing and praising just to be experiencing. You will wait every day to see what I will create for you. Life becomes exciting and joyous and filled with gratitude. The experience of one life will begin. It is fulfillment beyond your understanding. One word is needed to put your attention on now. That is 'stillness'. You find me, God and your higher selves in stillness.
Jesus

Message from Heaven #98

Do you want a new life? Do you want to feel in peace every minute and in a state of joy for life every day? What would you say if I told you that you had it already? You do already have complete peace and joy. Your unhealed pain is just covering it up. As time goes by, another loss, another disappointment, and another hurt of some kind accumulates this energy inside – all because you do not feel it rightly.

Your pain and the underlying fears that cause them are the only thing that prevents you from living fullness of life. You have been taught to avoid them and cover them up. This is the most damaging thing you could do to yourself. It puts shame on you; deep shame and pain. You learn not to accept yourself. You learn your natural feelings are bad and wrong. This makes **you** bad and wrong for being who you are.

You grow up feeling nothing that is real. Your life is a façade and you don't even know it. You are fully caught up in it by a young age. You have learned how to manipulate yourself. And you live and strive to be someone you are not. This brings ongoing heartache and pain to a point that you lose yourself before even knowing who you are to begin with.

Now what happens to your soul self? It becomes terribly suppressed by suppressing your feelings your whole life. It feels more and more sorrow and emptiness. Yes, your soul has feelings; more than you could know. It wants you to love it. When you become unhappy enough, you begin to seek inside of yourself for something more. The time frame from point A to here is so many lifetimes you couldn't count them; so many lifetimes of continued pain progressing. This is completely unnecessary. Lifetime after lifetime I watch you go down further. It is painful to see and to experience. All of this misery in one form to the next, until you are finally ready to give it all up; the resisting of your pain and fear.

You cannot escape it forever. You will one day need to face it. You created it unknowingly, but you still created it. Only you can forgive it. It is your illusory existence that you have to accept to let go of it. I cannot do this for you. I can only help you do this for yourself. You are empowered to create what you want.

Feel daunted not. What is beyond daunting is continuing to live with hiding the truth. Know that you have to face your truth to come home to your natural state of peace and joy. Mahavatar Babaji* specializes in facing the ego's pain and fear. He is a master at this. We have given you a method that makes it easier, much easier.

The *HOPE Technique* will get you to the source of your suppressed pain and fear effectively. You need to feel it to heal it and become free of it. It only hurts so much when you resist it. When you allow it, you can actually have peace with it. I repeat that there is only one thing blocking you from living your potential and that is your unhealed pain and fear. Use the *HOPE Technique*. Make it your daily priority. When there is no more fear left to resist, enlightenment comes in an instant. Then, my way of living arises automatically.
Jesus

Message from Heaven #99

When you start crying your heart out, you are healing your pain and fear. Avoiding this keeps it all within you. This diminishes your state of awareness and experience greatly. It suppresses your love and joy and peace. Are you ready to begin healing? You can continue to delay it. But, that would

---
* Spiritual teacher, Mahavatar Babaji, who Jesus refers to as his "right hand man"

be a shame of lost joy for life. When you are ready to face and feel your pain, the joyous life you are meant to experience is right around the corner.

Courage is required to face your pain. I will be bringing you people in the near future that can assist you with doing the *HOPE Technique*. Some of you may not feel strong enough to face it alone initially. I will bring you all the help you need to grow. But, know that feeling your pain can truly be easy. It just takes a little practice at first. All you need is the willingness to sit with it a little bit each day.

Each and every suppressed pain from more than a lifetime will come out of you, literally, again and again. Doing the *HOPE Technique* prevents you from staying stuck in it. You get through it without judgment. It is the judgment of your pain that makes it hurt so much. The *HOPE Technique* is going to be known world-wide. It is a way back to realizing your true self.

I know you are afraid to feel your pain but, know I am with you through it. You will have what you need to get past it with your willingness. Freedom is on the other side; a freedom you do not yet know. I wish I could give you the experience of it without going through this process, but that is not possible. I cannot take away what you create and want to hang onto. But, I can help you through it and I will. Know this.

Jesus

A Wave of Darkness

Message from Heaven #100

Now that some of you understand more the importance of healing your emotional pain, I'd like to talk about something new. A wave of darkness is coming to earth. It will cover the globe. I know you may not want to think of it, but remember that hiding from truth is not going to prevent it. Facing the truth will give you freedom from your fear.

How you choose to face your fear is what is most important. You can make it worse or you can make it a positive. Facing your fear in a healthy way is not being negative; it is the opposite. Honor it with integrity. This means with honesty and a positive mind set. This means to make it a benefit.

A mass destruction is coming to this planet. It is inevitable. It has already been created. There is no reversing it at this point. Know that God always turns your errors into a blessing. You will not wake up without this blessing from our Father. He wants to put an end to the planetary suffering.

I have discussed the need for building self-sufficient communities. Now, I want to discuss the need for a healing facility in every one of these. Connie is going to help bring together my first community and healing facility. I invite you all to copy it. This will bring a new way of living to the world that you cannot bring about on your own. This way of living supports spiritual growth. There will be no name associated with it but love. Maybe you cannot distort the concept of the word love. Leave the name God out of it; that will only mess it up. Love is what our Father is made of - pure love. Do not think anything more about it. That keeps you stuck in defining it and then your beliefs become your 'everything' and separate you from one another.

Leave your beliefs out of it please. Put your attention on loving each other. This is the only thing you need to know – ever.

I would like a healing facility in each community. They will be needed. You all need to heal to grow. Make the *HOPE Technique* the primary purpose of the healing facility. But, also bring helpful knowledge to all, including any passers-by. Give them the knowledge I am sharing. Love them all. Support them all. They are your brothers and sisters. Never forget this. Know that they have all helped you at one time. You have all been together before, again and again. It is another time to bring each other love.

When you hear of a new government coming, claiming they will help all of you to be given more, know this is not in alignment with my way of living. I support your freedom. Anyone that takes this away is not to be trusted. What is your freedom? I will explain this in specific detail.

Being self-sufficient is one way of freedom. Self-sufficiency with your survival needs. Do not put yourself in the position of relying on any government for your survival needs. You are meant to live in groups, so you can share your gifts, living in love and harmony. Living solo is not natural nor is it even possible in the long term. A ruling government is not considered a loving and caring group to me. Be able to support yourselves fully within each small community.

Freedom to have your own beliefs is necessary. You are fighting God's world if you want others to have your own beliefs. You were not made to be the same in every way. This includes your beliefs. Honor each other's beliefs. This is a freedom.

Making decisions for yourself is necessary for freedom. This can get turned into a gray area. Keep it simple. What you choose to eat or do to yourself is your own freedom. Make no judgments about another's personal choices. Learn for yourselves what feels right for you. This is sometimes different than another's.

The freedom to live happily and in peace is necessary. This means a life style that supports spiritual growth. This also means a balanced life style. Keep this simple also. Do not get into deciding for others what you think is healthy for them. Keep these opinions to yourself. Just be free to live a balanced and healthy life that allows for spiritual growth. Remember that putting your attention on growing spiritually will automatically bring balance to everything. Simply, support this for one another.

Freedom to teach and to learn what you want to support is another freedom. Allow each other to learn what they want for themselves. This is simple.

Children need their families back. Do not take over the parent's place. Children need guidance and direction from their parents, families and friends. To clarify this more, do not allow any government to raise your children or make decisions for them.

Freedom to live in a healthy and clean earthly environment is needed. Support nothing that poisons yourselves and the earth.

Freedom to be at one with me means taking all of these suggestions and making them one. Please keep it simple.
Jesus

Message from Heaven #101

Before you get fearful, don't. It's time to let go of it. Become the powerful beings you are. There is nothing to fear if you are in a state of wanting God. I am all you need. Change your habitual fearful thinking. Just surrender it to me every time it comes up. It is the power in your fear that actually manifests precisely that which you fear.

If you fear being betrayed, you will unconsciously attract people and experiences in which you are betrayed. If you fear the devil, evil trickery will be bestowed on you in one way or another. If you fear poverty, you will eventually experience poverty. You will experience every fear you hang onto until they are all fully healed.

These experiences come to you to help you face those fears you have been avoiding. Your fears are not in alignment with your true-self, your soul. Know that there is one fear from which all other fears are created. You can stop this unconscious pattern by doing the *HOPE Technique*. I will give you further instructions for how to surrender your fear effectively:

Whatever you fear, face it in your mind. Experience it fully in your head; the worst case scenario. Where would you end up? Living homeless on the street? Dying alone in a hospital? Experiencing the loss of a loved one? Getting fired from your job? Perhaps being hungry or even starving? Being humiliated in front of your friends? Being deceived and cheated on? Go ahead and think of all the experiences you fear. Experience them in your head until the feeling of resistance is no more. Then move on to the next one. Do this until there are no more fears left to experience. Face them head on. What happens then? You don't care about it anymore. It just dissolves. You'll go where you need to go, which is where you are not feeling fearful anymore. It's as simple as this.

It seems almost too simple, doesn't it? Simple solutions for complicated problems always work best. Once you can face your fears like this, they will disappear. It is the nature of life. What you avoid and resist grows stronger. What you face head on weakens and fades away. You will grow past your fear quickly by doing this.
Jesus

Message from Heaven #102
Can all of you come together in my name? Not to talk at all, but to simply come together for me? To tell yourselves silently that you want to experience more of me and that you are devoting your lives to our Father; that you are ready to serve God and each other; that you are ready to grow spiritually and make this your priority; that you are ready to make any needed changes and to welcome them. Then, think of nothing and just send me your love. Make it a silent gathering. All of you coming together for one purpose – to expand your loving energy; to bring a smile to your heart thinking of me.

Devotion is another topic I'd like to talk about. I have discussed it little. But there is nothing more significant than your devotion. Devotion is love felt and intentionally sent outward. It is a high honor to give and receive it. There is nothing stronger than giving your devotion. It's the giving of yourself to another.

Giving your devotion to God creates a very special connection like no other. It is the beginning of a new love when you are giving devotion to God. Loving in a devoted way is unconditional. You give love wanting nothing

back for it. It is the purest form of love. It is love given without wanting anything in return. This level of loving is the highest. You cannot just do it overnight. It requires cultivating. It cannot be strived for nor forced upon to be created. It happens spontaneously. Having the desire to serve God is how it gets started and you can begin this first before actually feeling total, genuine devotion.
Jesus

Message from Heaven #103

I'd like to ask all of you something else. It may sound impractical at first. But, remember that until you are fully established in unity consciousness, some of my suggestions may not seem to make sense. Still, they will promote the development of your consciousness.

Many actions expand your soul's awareness within your consciousness. Yet, they are not valued until the benefits become experienced. The mind works in a way opposite from the soul. The mind is all about itself. The soul is all about everything.

Choose to be of service, to help someone you do not already know; a person or an animal. Then, make the commitment to help this being for one hour a week. You are going to give him/her your personal one-on-one time for an hour each week. This hour is solely for them. It is to help them be happier.

When you are done with your hour of time for them, say a short prayer for them to our Father. Ask our Father to help them grow closer to God's love, peace and joy and to bring them more of what they need. Bring your heart felt desire for them to God. Tell our Father you are grateful for your ability to serve and help this other being.
Jesus

Message from Heaven #104

Many are waiting to grow into being a more loving person. In your busy world, this is not practical. You are caught up in a chaotic system of living that has forgotten that loving is your life line. It is what gives you everything good. For some of you, your output of giving love is barely there. This brings consequences. Everything you think, feel and do brings consequences to the giver. Through the power you have to create, you are the receiver of everything you give.

When you begin to consciously want to give more love to others, a power you know not of begins to ignite. It is a power beyond your understanding. This power blossoms within you in feelings of increased peace, love and joy, compassion, forgiveness, excitement for life and a stronger desire to give more love continues to grow. In time, you get it; you connect the dots. You realize that the happiness and joy you've been striving for your whole life is found in the acts of giving happiness and joy to others. The world begins to makes sense. Freedom enters your inner and outer world. A new found love for creation is born. It is a love you know not yet that brings true fulfillment. It is the beginning of experiencing truth. The feeling of comfort from being at home in your chaotic world starts to be experienced. A peace that passes all understanding is in your direct experience now and your whole world is completely different.

This new way of living comes spontaneously. The need to accomplish anything for yourself fades away into non-existence. You begin to attract more than you ever could have wanted for yourself in all ways, including abundance in the physical world. Healing occurs within you that may not be understood. You witness a power that is healing you which is greater than you alone. You surrender to it gladly with excitement and joy and gratitude. You are now letting your Creator take over. From here, words cannot explain the love that enters your life.
Jesus

Message from Heaven #105
Become the all-powerful beings you are through me. Give me your desires. Give them to me consciously. Give them to me and ask me to take care of them for you. Doing this one suggestion alone will change your world more toward harmony, miracles and inner joy.

What happens when you do this? I am given your permission to come into your desire. Through me, you will receive all of your needs. Trust begins the moment you ask me to take over your desires. I want to help you more than you know. If you ask me for help, but then fight to create without me, I am no longer handling it for you. If you take back your will to fight your way through life, I take a back seat and wait on you. It is that simple.

Giving me your desires means you let go of them. It is a surrendering of trying to create what you want. Give me the desire and give up your fruitless fight. Your desire is all that I need.

Jesus

Message from Heaven #106

I am a presence that you can feel and many of you are feeling my presence more. It begins with a little more peace, then hope and then a feeling of more trust begins to replace fear and doubt. Your thoughts change and your mind begins thinking of my love. Ever so gradually, more love starts to enter your conscious awareness. You find yourself thinking of others more and honor their feelings as your own. It is usually subtle at first. You may not even realize it for a little while.

Then, you get ideas about living your life differently, including doing more for others. The desire comes naturally. Your own desires seem not so important anymore. You transition your thinking spontaneously more to what you can give and less to what you can get. You feel something within you start to wake up. It is a beautiful feeling.

Then all of a sudden, awareness expands and you 'get it'. You comprehend the meaning of your life. You realize there is a purpose in your life that you never thought of before. Excitement for life becomes a new found experience. Inner joy develops and you intentionally change your life. You realize what does not fit with who you are anymore; what is holding you back from growth, happiness, fulfillment. Your priorities change and your life is reorganized. As time goes by, you become more humble. This makes you more open to others who you were closed off to before. And right about this time, you become more open to receiving a more awakened presence of who you really are. Now, you begin living for me instead of only yourself.

This is when bigger miracles occur, seemingly by happenchance. But, know you have now entered my way of life. Power becomes you. There is power in your thoughts, words and actions unlike before. Now you know why you are here. You begin to experience the divine in every part of your life. Gratitude blossoms within you. It is completely new. An inner joy and awe for life becomes your predominant feeling. You change people's lives in a significant way and are a part of life like never before. You know you are here for me and you are so happy to find this out.

Freedom from the stresses in life are reduced to nothing and you are now living a different life. You strongly want to live for me. We become one mind, one heart, one soul, one life. We are in the process of unifying; merging as one. A new love enters your direct experience that cannot be explained. Any words will limit it, but it is a love and a joy that is a miracle beyond human understanding. The love within you becomes a powerful presence. You are not your single self anymore. You are all that is.
Jesus

Message from Heaven #107

I know many of my words may seem over exaggerated and I understand why you are hurting inside sometimes when you read them. Reading my words brings more awareness to all that you are missing. At first, there is a little or a lot of fear involved with this. You are afraid of being forgotten by God. You are afraid of being left out. Fears come to the surface with thoughts about God. There is a deep guilt and shame with your connection to me. You do not understand why, yet it is there.

Many of you will close the door at this point, wishing to hear no more. It is frightening. The pain inside of you gets stirred up just by reading my words because what you need to forgive is what holds you back and you want to avoid it. Stagnation feels more comfortable and far safer.

I want you to become more open hearted. The opening of your heart initially brings the pain and it may not seem a desirable process. The emptiness within you that has always been there for no apparent reason is due to your fears. This disconnection with your Creator begins at birth and continues through life, but you do not understand why. You try to fill the incomplete feeling with something else, usually for a very long time.

This seeking is an unconscious yearning for something to fulfill you. If you knew what was on the other side of your pain, you would be happy and excited to face it. In time, you would realize it was never real to begin with.

Know that I love you. Know that you are not incomplete or missing anything. Know that self-forgiveness is needed to find your way back to me. Seek to forgive yourself from your illusory misgivings, imperfections and mistakes from the past. Remind yourself daily that there is no such thing as being separated from your Creator. Just remind yourself of this. You could not exist if you were not God. He is already within you fully. Seek to heal your pain and fear. Your wholeness is always there. It is your unhealed pain and fear that distorts your experience. Face your pains from the past. Do not carry them anymore. Forgive them by doing the *HOPE Technique*.
Jesus

Message from Heaven #108

My way of living induces the expansion of more love, which heals and reduces the fear. Simply put, your Source of love grows inside. It is always there waiting to be realized and expressed, but more fear must first leave to allow room for it. It is that simple. You become more love and less fear in everything about you. Your thoughts, your perception, your desires and your behaviors become more loving.

With increased loving comes increased peace, happiness and true fulfillment. You feel more and more at home. Confusion is replaced with clarity and wisdom. Simply put, you become more loving like me.

You can **intentionally** induce this natural process of growing your soul. You simply try to live like me. You go beyond yourself and think of how you can add more love, healing and happiness into the lives of others and then you do it. It is so simple. **Wanting** to do this is challenging at first. You do not see the benefit in it for you. But, you will never know the benefits until you begin to do it.

So then, pain becomes a part of your life. It comes from what you don't do as much as from what you do. I just want you to know this. Pain is not a necessary criterion for enlightenment. Suffering comes in many forms, all from your lack of consciousness of the love that you are. God will bring you whatever you need to unify with Him. He wants you back.
Jesus

Message from Heaven #109

Giving more of yourself requires a letting go of yourself. It is the last thing your ego-mind wants to do. In fact, your present perception will instantly become threatened with the notion of giving more of what you have. This includes your energy in all possible ways; your thoughts, your feelings, your time, your actions, your possessions and your desires. You want to keep everything you have for yourself. The thought of giving anything away that you value, for nothing in return, is initially unpleasing. Your mind thinks that if it gives away something it values, it will have less of it. This makes logical sense. There is an automatic resistance in your perception about giving away something you value.

You can see this perception easily in a young child's way of thinking and behaving. A child can play with his toy and enjoy it for a little while. But, he will become bored in time without anyone else to share his experience. The child will learn that sharing what he has brings a much deeper and richer and joyful experience. This develops self-love and fulfillment.

One can be an adult without being grown up yet. In fact, growing up and maturing spiritually has nothing to do with one's age. It has to do with one's heart. When the heart grows, one is growing up spiritually. Self-centeredness becomes less and less because the qualities that come from the heart are replacing the mind's self-centered perception with a unity-centered perception.

Being thoughtful to others – their feelings, their needs, their desires, their level of happiness starts to become of more interest to you when you start to develop your heart. A significant transition from self-centered thinking to unity-thinking can occur after experiencing extreme loss and despair. It does not matter what set of circumstances get you to this place. What matters is that you get to the point where this transformation starts to take place. This is when you start developing the God within you. This is when you start to grow spiritually at a faster pace.

You can bypass the need to experience this loss and despair if you are willing to start living for others before reaching this time that induces this transition in your perception from self to others. You usually do not do this willingly. You do this when you are so broken, lost and confused, you simply let go of yourself because you cannot keep fighting life for what you want anymore. You become too exhausted and give up because you cannot continue living in the same way. Getting to this place is a slow, painful route. Know it is a completely unnecessary route when you are willing to allow this transition to take place.

You can put the cart before the horse, so to speak, and prevent this need by intentionally thinking of other's feelings, desires and needs. Put your thought energy in the form of action behind it. Start doing acts that help others be healthier, happier and more cared for. You will start receiving the benefits even though you may not be doing these things with a fully developed genuine desire for them yet. Still, you will induce the expansion of your heart's love regardless. You will grow spiritually. And, in time, you will begin to realize you need never think about what you need or want. You leave that to your divine Creator.

You start experiencing more of God, which is loving energy. It, God, starts taking care of everything in your life more effectively than you ever could have on your own with your self-centered way of thinking. Induce this transition from ego-perception to a more loving and unified perception by letting go of your desires, your wants and start living for other's happiness and fulfillment. It is this simple. In a short time, you will start feeling our Father awaken within you and you will naturally come to want more of Him more than anything else. He will continue to expand and grow within you and He will take care of everything for you.

Jesus

Message from Heaven #110

Self-centeredness is a perception that is all about self – your human self and what you can gain from the physical world. It is not wrong to want more joy, abundance and pleasurable experiences from the material world. You are here to enjoy what the physical world has to offer.

But, living your lives solely or mostly for what you can experience from the physical world is not going to fulfill you – ever. In fact, the more you gain in the physical world, the more you will become discontent **if** you are not also growing spiritually. Temporary excitement for what you gain in the physical world can be fun, but it is limited. Striving for more becomes compulsive and fear will expand within your consciousness. This eventually turns into attracting painful experiences in one form or another.

It is God – the God within you, letting you know that you are forgetting what is vitally important - Him; the God within you. This means your Source of love energy. This energy literally flows through your soul and heart. You have full access to this God energy and can use it to create your life without the effort of your conscious mind. In fact, this intelligent and creative God energy will do a better job at creating fullness of life for you than you could ever accomplish on your own without Him.

I would like to entice you to turn your life over to the care of God **before** you have the natural, genuine desire or interest in doing so. It usually takes an enormous amount of pain and suffering to get one to a place where they **want** to do this. But you do not have to go through a long painful phase to begin wanting God to take over your life. You can simply ask Him to now, which means, you need to put action behind your asking Him - you start living for **what you think God would want you to do**. You just start thinking of Him and what you think He would like you to do today, this hour, this minute. Remember that "Him", our Father, is your love.

This transitions your entire life to living for God - Love. This is devotion to God - to love. This is your soul self. Doing it well or not so well, matters not. It is your heart's desire, your willingness and intention to respond with love that brings an end to feeling incomplete and needing more loss and pain to point you in the right direction.

Jesus

Soul Awareness

Message from Heaven #111

GAIN MORE AWARENESS of your soul.
Jesus

Message from Heaven #112

There are two ways to reach enlightenment, that is, God consciousness. It is through intentional development of your soul's awareness or unintentional development of your soul's awareness.

I will remind you that as you develop your soul's awareness, you are simultaneously healing your heart from your accumulated pain and fear. They are one and the same. Your soul's love expands within your heart as you heal away your heart's pain and fear. I have highly suggested doing the *Heart Technique* and the *HOPE* Technique daily to accomplish this quicker and easier.

That being said, I have also given you many other suggestions for how to intentionally develop your soul's awareness by means of altering the energy you give out; the energy from your own thoughts, feelings and actions. When I say "feelings", I am referring to more love-based feelings and less fear-based feelings.

Your thoughts and actions create the quality of your feelings. So, if you think more like me and perform actions more like mine, you will develop more love-based feelings. This develops more awareness of your soul. Your soul is your Source of unconditional love and it is our Father. **Your soul's love is our Father.** This is what you want to experience more of; this is what you are here for. Know that our Father is experienced through your human form; through a developed heart.

If you start adding more of my way of thinking, which simply means more loving thoughts, and you start performing more of my way of behaving (actions/living), you will start feeling more as I do. This means more like the God within you. Until you start experiencing and feeling the benefits of thinking and behaving more like me, you cannot know the fulfillment this will give you. I am referring to the presence of the love, joy and peace of God; God is fully within you already. You have only forgotten this because your pain and fear predominates.

So, I want to help you understand that you can induce the expansion of the love that you are, into your conscious awareness by **intentionally** thinking more loving thoughts and performing more loving actions. I want to further emphasize that doing this may initially not seem so valuable to you. But, I'd like you to do it anyway.

Choosing to do this intentionally develops your soul's awareness. After doing this for a little while, you will come to know its' value and you will then never want to stop doing it. Simply put, it is intentionally waking up your soul. You are the one that surrenders intentionally and it is only you who can. I am then able to help you much more.
Jesus

Message from Heaven #113

Are you going to hear my words and do something with them? What are you going to do that is different? Are you too busy to change your life and world? It will be changed either way, but I'd like you to be among the healers and rebuilders.

Every day that goes by is another day to create your own freedom; freedom from trials and tribulations, fear and despair, lack and limitation. Have you thought about what you are going to do today? Who do you not yet know who is on your list to help in some way? Will you look for someone to help today? Or will you be engulfed in yourself? Also, can you spend some time in silence with me? Will you?

The changes you are waiting for in your world must be created by you. You are given the freedom to do what you will. May all of you listen well to your hearts. Your minds are your guide most of the time but you can turn this around with intention. In a short time you will begin to feel what you are gaining and it is no longer a challenge giving to others for nothing obvious in return.
Jesus

Message from Heaven #114

I am going to give a practical message; how to schedule a little time for your soul today. If you seem stuck in your busy day without me, baby steps are needed. Do not judge yourself for this. The whole world is caught up in busyness. A powerful momentum from the collective makes it seem challenging to change it.

I will say this – you only need to change your priorities to make it simple and easy. But let's begin with a couple baby steps for those who need it. How about starting with two things first. An hour a week to bring more happiness to someone and, three 5 minute increments of connecting with me each day - just for me. Choose a person or animal or the earth. Get an hour scheduled next week for him/her/it. Give him/her/it an hour of your time in love and care. Make this a habit. Morning, afternoon and night, spend five minutes with me talking silently. Connect with me intentionally. Tell me how you are feeling and what you need help with today. Tell me what you are grateful for. End this time saying my prayer (#27) to our Father. This will be a good start for now.

Let's reiterate to keep it clear and simple:

1. Donate 1 hour of your time each week to bring increased happiness to someone, or an animal, or your planet earth.
2. Silently connect with me for 5 minutes, three times each day [morning, afternoon, evening]. Tell me how you are feeling, what you need help with and what you are grateful for.
3. End each of these 3 sessions by saying my prayer [#27] to our Father:

Message from Heaven #27 A PRAYER FROM JESUS:
"I am here to ask You, my Creator for a deeper and stronger connection to the Love that You are. I am ready to add more of Your awareness into my conscious awareness. I feel incomplete without You. I feel an emptiness without You. I feel fear without You. My world is a limited world without awareness of You. The less love in my heart, the less aware I am of You. Living life without full awareness of You brings painful experiences. The pain is there to get my attention and let me know something is missing and incomplete. I have lost the understanding of why we experience pain. The entire world has forgotten this."

"I want You back in my conscious awareness and direct experience in life. Nothing can fulfill me as You can. I want You back. Please show me how I can live a life more in accordance with unifying as one heart, one mind and one soul again. I am lost without You Father. I love You and want to grow closer to You."
Jesus

Message from Heaven #115

Let's now begin developing your soul directly. The *Heart Technique* is a practice that taps into your soul directly. It awakens your soul intentionally. There is a sequence of silent actions done during this time of practice. It is a perfect sequence of steps which enhance each other. First, still the mind, then feel your soul, then self-forgiveness comes into it; then, an intentional creation. Lastly, there is gratitude for life. It is a simple, yet powerful spiritual practice for thirty-five minutes daily.

This will be a big commitment for some; perhaps even daunting. Thirty-five minutes a day doing 'nothing' may seem impractical. But, know this: you need to give your soul some time to allow it to take over your life. Your soul can and will fulfill your needs for you. And, will do so much better than your mind's ego if you allow it. The transformation that awaits you can only be given from your soul. It is much more than you know.

If you want me, freedom from limitations and unification with our Creator, you must grow your soul. It is as simple as that.
Jesus

Message from Heaven #116

When you have comfortably established the daily habit of practicing the *Heart Technique*, it is time for effective and thorough emotional healing by doing the *HOPE Technique*. Schedule a best time to do the *HOPE Technique* allowing a half hour of your time. At times you may feel finished with your emotional healing after a few minutes, sometimes much longer. But, allow yourself all the time you need to complete the cycle naturally.

Emotional healing from your many past hurts and developed fears is what will fully set you free. All limitations in your life experiences are in your mind and body. They are a direct result of 'stored' pain and fears. You will never be free of them without facing and feeling them. Doing the *HOPE Technique* daily will quickly get you past them. This daily habit of effectively healing and releasing more pain and fear will change your life in every way imaginable. You will come to know who you are underneath all of that pain and fear. Enlightenment is inevitable when you are healing what blocks your true self from shining through and being realized (*HOPE Technique*), and when you are intentionally expanding your soul (*Heart Technique*).

Implementing these two daily practices into one's life is a new way of living. I am introducing this to the world now. It is the knowledge you need to achieve God-realization in a relatively short period of time.
Jesus

Message from Heaven #117

When you are established in the daily habit of practicing the *HOPE Technique* and the *Heart Technique*, you will be growing spiritually at a rapid rate. In a short time, you will begin to feel more and more happy and peaceful in your every waking moment. Imbalances and limitations dissolve away. Your soul begins to create your life for you. Ease and grace becomes

your every moment experience. A new life awaits you - literally. I have been waiting for this time of expansion of your heart and soul a very long time. I will be with you along your journey of connecting to me more and more. In time, we will not be separate in your conscious awareness. Remember to enjoy the present along the way.
Jesus

Message from Heaven #118

When you become more deeply established in enlightenment, which means the awakening of your soul's love, you start feeling a strong desire to help the world. Instead of trying to help a few people at a time, you begin to think of the whole world, including the earth. You want to promote miraculous shifts in the world's consciousness. You have incredible support from God to accomplish this – all from your own love. You become a very powerful presence on earth. I'd like to talk more about this – your power and precisely what that means.

There is a force, an energy, with the power of God; with the power of the love you are animating out from within your body. It is a magnificent power. It is an intelligent power. It is a power that cannot be described in any language for this is truly indescribable. But, it is a power, a force and an intelligence that is masterfully creative and all-knowing. It creates constantly. It creates from what it is given. The more energy it is given, the more powerful its ability to create. Your consciousness, that is your awareness which includes your desires and intentions, intertwines with this power and your desires and intentions become extremely powerful. The world moves for your desires and intentions and it does so automatically. You do not do it; the power does it. Your desire is what guides it. The more your desires are in alignment with this power, the more the desires are supported. As you begin to learn your relationship with this power, it continues to increase. It never stops increasing.

There is a feeling that accompanies this power. It is the most divine feeling; pure love, pure peace, pure stillness, pure unity consciousness. This is home. This is our home; the only home in all of existence.

There are also special abilities that accompanies one when their inner power comes to a certain point of fullness. Many humans do not know of these abilities. I'd like to talk more about these abilities that develop spontaneously when one's power becomes magnified. These abilities are going to start developing quickly when there is much less collective fear energy on the planet; some you may have heard about and some you have not.

It is true that you have all the abilities within you that I do. They are presently dormant. There is not enough power flowing through your consciousness. In time, when there is more, you will develop powers; the power to create like never before. You will heal the earth from your damage. You will do it adeptly. The love in your hearts will surge with a power due to the decrease of planetary fear energy. You will be able to spend a few moments or less sending a section of the earth love, and it will come to life extremely quickly.

I am telling you this because there will be a time when you will not feel your power. You will not know what you have available. It is my healing power I am talking about. I will bring life to the deadened earth through your hearts. You will all grow quickly and create a new earth.
Jesus

Message from Heaven #119

Why not try to maximize your power now. With love in your heart, it is possible. I am referring to the power to create what your love wants. When your love is for another, there is no limitation in the power to manifest into a physical creation. If you can sit quietly and still your mind's thoughts, your love can emerge with intention. You have no agenda and no specific cause but to increase the output of your loving energy. You leave it to God what to do with your love. You send others loving, caring energy and wishes. You simply feel love for them and send them your wish for their fulfillment. You wish for their happiness and peace. You can even see them with a happy heart. If you all did this for only a few minutes a day to someone other than yourself, there would be no more wars nor despair nor illness nor dysfunction. Why not try it? This love you send out will come back to you ten-fold.

Getting out of the ego's habit of self-centered thinking is challenging without the conscious desire for it. It is a slow process. This slow process can be turned around to a short time with intention. You can claim your life back instead of living in an unconscious pattern of thought and behavior. You only need to have the desire.
Jesus

Message from Heaven #120
Many of you are yearning for a place to call home; yearning to feel at home. You do not feel at home anywhere. You feel displaced. You do not feel like you fit into this world. A pain of sorrow develops that can turn into bitterness and resentment. This happens because you cannot get the fullness, the comfort, the sense of belonging your heart is seeking. It is the reuniting with its' Maker that it is yearning for. But, you ignore its' calling and continue to feel more unworthy of love as a result. This means you feel more and more undeserving of God's love. Then a bitterness and resentment specifically toward God can develop.

This is when a phase of more loss and challenges enter your life. You do not consciously understand that **you** are turning away from the only thing that will fill you with the fullness you are seeking. So a frustration enters your experience. It is a hurting heart from feeling unimportant to God. Bitterness, frustration and resentment grows and becomes a greater part of who you are. It helps to cover up the fear. This underlying feeling that each and every one of you will develop is a hurt that is not real, but feels real. This feeling is from the fear of not being good enough for God's love. This occurs because you already feel separate from God. It is a distorted perception. It is not real. But, nonetheless, it **feels** real.

Every one of you will get to this point of dissatisfaction with God or life. This causes anger toward God or life. You also often blame it on a person or situation. It is all the same fear; fear that God does not love you. Life becomes increasingly painful now. You spontaneously attract more challenges. Your soul is creating bigger obstacles to get your attention to what you are missing – devotion to God. Devotion to God is lost. Your heart's love wants its love returned. But, you avoid looking to yourself for the answer to all of your problems. Dysfunction becomes rampant in every aspect of your life. Your soul is crying out for attention. It is saying, *"look to Me, I am what you need"*. Yet, you usually ignore that. You fear your own soul because it is unknowable to the mind. The need to be made willing is now vital. You will attract something to bring you to your knees; a place of surrendering your painful feelings.

Please understand that you could stop this entire process now, before getting to this level of despair and emptiness. Start living for me instead of for yourself. It is so easy.
Jesus

The Second Coming is Through Your Heart

Message from Heaven #121

MANY ARE WONDERING if I am coming back on earth for you. I am. What you call the "second coming" is not through my own physical body again, but through yours - through your heart and consciousness – through **your** body. I am your Savior, but I only come to those who want me. I never force myself on anyone. Following God must be wanted.

There is a lot of knowledge about myself that I leave unspoken for now. I only give you knowledge that you are ready to receive; that you are capable of accepting. I want to enhance your capacity for knowing more. This type of knowing is not through the mind, but through the heart. I am waiting for your hearts to develop further.

For many of you the cycle of your mind is habitual. It is on automatic; busyness to a maximum before complete insanity. That is what comes soon for many of you if you do not slow down your thinking. Practice a daily meditation that effectively stills the mind's thoughts so you have the ability to grow further. You are all trapped in your minds right now and you do not know it. This already defines insanity.
Jesus

Message from Heaven #122

Some of you think you know me because you are a Christian. I want to expand your thinking to being more in alignment with mine. I was not a Christian. I was not a separate "anything". Belief systems often create division, not unity. Honor me and my teachings without separating yourselves

from others. There are not even as few as two Christians who believe everything exactly the same. Remember that you unify with me more when you make loving your priority rather than your beliefs. Also, remember that beliefs come from the mind but it is through the heart that you experience me. Honor your beliefs and each others, but do not define yourselves from your beliefs. This will limit your connection to our Father. Put your attention on loving one another rather than judging everyone's worthiness by your beliefs. Do not try to convert another's beliefs to be more like yours. This keeps you stuck in separation. I did not care about people's many beliefs. I cared about making them happy and whole again, uniting them with our Father's love. I honored and accepted all. Please remember this.
Jesus

Message from Heaven #123
I'd now like to discuss others who have different religious beliefs. I want to help you create unity and a united religious belief; a belief that honors all beliefs equally. This will promote unity. Your attention and awareness will go beyond your beliefs from the mind and you will become more involved in the action of loving. All religious beliefs are honored by me. I already know you are not your beliefs. I want you to know that what you call yourself makes no difference to our true connection.
Jesus

Message from Heaven #124
Before you get defensive, think about my words for a minute. Who do you think you are? A name? A title? A profession? A religion? A different "other"? Who are you? Who do you represent? You think your mind's beliefs create your identity. I tell you otherwise. Your mind's thoughts and beliefs are temporary. They exist while you are in a human body. Who are you after you are not in a body anymore? Do you simply vanish to non-existence?

You fight and argue and struggle to define yourself and you lose your true Self in the process. You lose God in the process. You are making your

temporary beliefs more important than your life and our Father. This is a pity. Wake up from this separating of yourselves with others. Who are you beneath all that - all the labels and titles and names? These are no more than words. They hold no significance. You are not your beliefs. Who is beyond your beliefs? The 'who' which is real. I am referring to the 'you' before you were born; the 'you' who continues after your body is gone; the formless 'you'; the true 'you' that is eternal. This 'you' is all. Do not separate yourself for the sake of a temporary belief.
Jesus

Message from Heaven #125
Before you allow your ego to take you back to a more negative state so that it can feel more comfortable and safe, I'd like to expand your understanding of the ego's identity. This will help you understand more about energy; the energy that is within you which governs your entire life.

Your modern science already understands that every cell in your body is living, moving energy that changes constantly. Moment to moment, it never stays the same. Every atom in your universe consists of living, moving, always changing energy. What does this mean? It means that who you are is energy and the quality of this energy can be more loving energy or more negative (fearful) energy. The quality of your energy creates what you attract and experience in your world. Peaceful, joyful and fulfilling experiences come into your life when you **feel** peaceful, joyful and fulfilled. When you feel stressed, with diminished joy, peace and love, you are attracting experiences that will continue to diminish your joy, peace and love. It is actually extremely simple. To reiterate - the more joyful, peaceful and loving your energy, the more joyful, peaceful and loving the experiences you will attract.

You can deliberately change your energy, the energy in every cell of your body, to being a higher quality of energy. So, creation energy will create more of what you want – more inner peace, joy and fulfillment. What controls your energy right now? Your perception. What is your perception? It is what you *think* is real. It is what you *believe* to be so. It is what your mind chooses to believe. It is your mind's identity; your ego. Your perception consists of many beliefs, all coming from your mind.

Your true self, your soul self, does not care about what your mind believes. It is irrelevant to it. Your soul knows your mind's beliefs are not real to begin with. Your soul knows your perception is a conglomeration of many beliefs that are temporary and always changing. It is simply the nature of it.

The soul cares about what you **feel**. It wants you to feel fully loving, like me. It wants to expand and grow into fullness. What you **feel** every moment is what governs your soul's ability to expand or to be restricted. Right now, your mind's beliefs control your feelings, rather than the other way around. This means your mind controls your life and world. Remember that your mind is a perception which changes according to what you believe. It is a temporary identity, forever changing; it is not your true, everlasting, invincible and unconditional loving identity.

You are here on earth to become and experience your true self, in your physical world. This means to grow past your mind's identity, which is limited to your ego's awareness. If you focus on your mind's beliefs as being 'everything', you live from your mind. As you focus on your feelings, you live more from your heart. Your heart is the path to uniting with our Father. This means how you **feel**, not what you **believe**.

So, paying more attention to your feelings and less attention to your beliefs is needed to grow closer to our Father. What does this mean? It means to be more aware of how you are feeling. It means to notice when you are feeling less than loving. The energy you want to induce is loving, harmonious and happy energy. **This means living more consciously than unconsciously.**
Jesus

Message from Heaven #126

I'd like to discuss something different… about Connie's prior experiences of higher states of awareness. It is time to share spiritual awakening experiences. So, I am asking Connie and all of you who have had an experience of the divine to please share your experience[s] with others (now on my "Messages from Heaven" Facebook page).

The experience of a higher state of awareness may be known as a 'divine' experience - without a shadow of a doubt. You know it is either an experience given to you directly from God or that it is a direct experience of God Himself. It will be helpful to share your experiences; it will help you and others grow by sharing your love and supporting each other's spiritual growth. Connect with each other in this way please.
Jesus

Message from Heaven #127

www.Facebook.com/HelpFromHeaven **is my new "Messages from Heaven" Facebook page.** I look forward to sharing our "spiritual awakening" experiences as Jesus suggested. I also invite you to share any particular life or spiritual-growth challenges you may be having or to ask Jesus any specific questions. I will share as many of your questions with Jesus' answers as I can. I look forward to connecting with you on Facebook this way. As Jesus said, we help each other to learn, heal and grow by sharing our experiences and supporting each other during our journey through life.
Love and Blessings, Connie

Message from Heaven #128

Experience of a Higher State of Consciousness (#1): What a time to have a "spiritual awakening". I lived near Stone Mountain in Atlanta, Georgia at the time and was then in corporate sales. Because I was between jobs, my daily lifestyle was conducive to spiritual growth. My habits were regular, including eating times and quality of food. There were no big stressors in my life.

My habit of smoking several cigarettes a day quickly and effortlessly dissolved away, as well as drinking a glass of wine a few nights a week (work days). I simply did not want cigarettes or wine anymore. My golden retriever and golden Labrador were the love of my life. We hiked together for a few hours each day. I faithfully meditated [Transcendental Meditation] twice daily, now had no 'bad' habits and had been a vegetarian most all of my life. (I am not a vegetarian now).

About a month earlier I had resigned from my job to relocate to Atlanta, and started practicing 10-15 minutes of simple yoga postures followed by 10 minutes of a simple breathing practice, pranayama, before both of my daily meditations. Also, because I had the additional time to invest in food preparation, I began a diet of about 75% raw foods and 25% cooked foods and a fresh raw veggie juice each morning. I was well-rested. Far gone were those typical 50+ hour high stress, high pressure work weeks.

During one particular morning meditation, I experienced what I can only call "bliss". This beautiful feeling of inner happiness and pure peace is truly beyond description. It was so overwhelming that tears were streaming down my cheeks. It was the most beautiful, comforting feeling I had ever experienced.

I was feeling extreme energy with what I can only define as lightness; un-heaviness and aliveness in my base chakra location (though I didn't know what chakras were at that time). It was like a wave of aliveness waking up inside of me. That aliveness-energy seemed to expand further up into my entire stomach area, then chest area and then my entire upper body and head. The only word I can come up with to describe this freeing feeling is bliss – extreme inner joy, a pure love and a pure peace. This was no doubt, a divine experience.

This feeling continued with me consistently for a few plus days. It was an absolute freedom from heaviness and limitation. It was an aliveness that no words can express. I was in love. Simply put, I was in love with myself, life and all that is. Not with anyone or anything in particular, but with everyone and everything. I felt that I WAS the love, bliss, peace energy. It was me and I was it.

I carried on about my day as usual. I was smiling a lot spontaneously. When I went to the store or on my usual daily walk in nature, or even filling up the tank at the gas station, I felt this deep, love and gratitude to everyone I saw around me. I knew without any doubt or even any thought, that we were directly connected. They were literally a part of me and I was a part of them. I knew this.

I had deep love and appreciation to them simply for existing and being exactly who they were. I somehow knew that their existence enabled me to be who I was and I had an automatic deep gratitude to them for it. I would have surrendered my life to them in a second with total devotion and love for them.

I had no fear of any kind. I knew I was immortal. I was in pure bliss. I was in love and had absolutely zero fear or worry about anything of any kind. The weight of my physical body felt incredibly light. I felt so alive, energized and of a pure freedom that is indescribable. It felt the extreme opposite of loneliness.

One afternoon, I was eating a plate of chopped fresh fruit. While I was bringing a bite of banana and a grape to my mouth with a fork, at that very second, I became one with that fruit. I had so much gratitude to the fruit for sharing itself with me and the fruit had so much gratitude to me for loving it, appreciating it and eating it.

The fruit was giving itself to me in total love and devotion and I was giving it my love and gratitude at the same time. I knew the fruit was literally a live being. It was not just a thing – a fruit. It was a live being. The fruit and I literally were one – totally connected and in ecstatic love with each other. (Yes, I know it sounds bizarre)

These few plus days I of course noticed how I did not have my usual worrisome thoughts about the need to find a job soon. My mind questioned this and I was intellectually puzzled. I thought to myself, "wow, I have absolutely no fear or worry about the fact that I need a job and still don't have one". I giggled in delight with this difference in my perception. I felt like an innocent, lighthearted child that didn't yet know what fear, judgment or worry was.

When at the grocery store I saw people around me and I noticed how I did not have usual judgmental thoughts about them, like judging how they were dressed, how they looked, what they represented, etc. I automatically loved them so very much and I felt like we were all literally very closely related blood-brothers and sisters.

I noticed when I was walking on a more isolated trail in the mountains with my dogs and I came upon a fellow walking in the area, I did not have reservations or thoughts about needing to be guarded, being in a somewhat vulnerable position out alone with a stranger and just myself. There was no such fear or reservations! I even intellectualized in my mind that if that man were a 'bad' guy and were to want to attack me or something, I would be happy to be a part of giving him an experience he needed.

There was nothing to fear regardless of what ever might happen. I would literally laugh out loud realizing there was nothing to fear! Everything was perfect no matter what. My existence was here for him as much as it was for me. I was in a place of automatic surrender to whatever was and could not feel fear in any way whatsoever. Such fear was simply not capable of being within my psyche or consciousness.

My mind would sometimes have the same thoughts that used to make me feel fearful, but there was no attachment to fear with these thoughts. It was like my feelings were not attached to or connected with my thoughts anymore. My thoughts did not control how I felt at all whatsoever and I intellectually recognized this difference. This was so incredibly interesting and intriguing to me, far beyond fascinating and liberating! I was at an inner state of awareness and direct experience of total freedom from all fear and judgments.

After a few plus days, this state of experience began to quickly fade as I was getting ready for a job interview. Within a few hours, I was back to my 'normal' state of awareness. The emptiness and lack of this love, peace, inner joy and freedom was a devastating disappointment. I was sobbing frequently for days after I lost this state of experience.

It was an extreme contrast and the loss with that was such a deep, painful loss. I yearned for that experience to come back more than words can describe. I felt so limited and separate again and I could do nothing for days but sob intensely, feeling the deepest pain imaginable of sorrow, emptiness and the loss of that love, freedom, joy, bliss and non-separation.

I got that job and started working a week later. It was beyond challenging trying to transition back to a very busy and stressful 50+ hour work week again doing something that was utterly meaningless to me. The contrast of activity was actually painful. I did not have another higher state of consciousness experience for years later.

Working again, I immediately got back into the daily grind of busy, stressful days with my job. I returned to fast food picked up on the run, waking up at 5 a.m. exhausted and dreading another long, hectic day of work ahead. I stopped doing my pranayama and yoga. A couple weeks later, I started smoking again.

Although, it was challenging as always to fit in a 45 minute meditation twice daily and required diligent daily discipline, I was used to this daily habit of maintaining my two daily meditations. I sacrificed my sleep and social life for it. I couldn't go out with friends after work as other people did if I were going to get in my second meditation. But, I consciously chose to make my meditations a priority.

What I didn't know then and knowing what I do now, I am certain this energy, this direct experience, was what Jesus refers to as the Father – the presence of God; the presence and awareness of our soul or higher self.

I will share about my next "spiritual awakening" experience soon and post. I hope you will also share some of your experiences on my *Messages from Heaven* Facebook page. I know that in the sharing of our experiences we can inspire and teach each other more.

Connie

Message from Heaven #129

Now that Connie has shared her first experience of a higher state of consciousness, I'd like to talk about it. I'd like to explain what happened and why. It is true that you must live a lifestyle that promotes a spiritual awakening in most cases. Your life energy, your spirit-self, is a certain quality of energy; loving and peaceful energy.

If you live in stressful, friction energy, you will inhibit your spirit energy from flowing through your body more fully. This reduces the quality of your thinking, feelings and actions. This reduces the quality of your life. What most of you think of as 'normal' is not. It is not 'normal' to feel less than fully loving, peaceful and joyful – although it is common. If you continue to live in a state of stress, then stress is what you get. Stress energy spills into every aspect of your life; physical health, emotional and mental well-being, your relationships, your financial condition, your level of inner peace and joy; the quality of your whole life.

I'd like to explain more about my desire for the building of communities and why I am recommending them. The quality of life on earth is declining. It has been declining for a long time. How can you create a healthier, more balanced, harmonious, loving, connecting life in an unhealthy, imbalanced, unharmonious, unloving, non-connecting world? You cannot. You need to create your own new life on earth.

Please create communities as I have previously described. These would be communities focused on loving, healing and rebuilding a new society together. This will positively influence all other life. Create a new way of life - a life that allows for and encourages spiritual growth. What Connie experienced is only a fraction of what is available. Our Father's love is beyond explanation. His love energy is being left out of your direct experience. Do you think you can experience more of His energy while continuing to live in stressful energy? You cannot. You need to reduce your stressful energy. To accomplish this, you must live less stressfully.

Also, know that it is not only how you spend your time or how much time is available for rest, relaxation and fun or enjoyable experiences. It is also ridding your body of stored stress from the past - the stored, accumulated pain and fear from past experiences. For this, practice the *HOPE Technique* and the *Heart Technique* daily.

Jesus

New Villages

Message from Heaven #130

Now that I have reiterated the importance of creating self-sustaining communities, I'd like to give you some practical guidance about how to get these communities started. Many of you are already interested in living a higher quality of life yet do not know how to create one. I will say first, make this desire clear in your mind and heart and consciously give it to God. Let Him figure it all out. Doing this – surrendering your desires to God - is what brings His power into your desire. That being said, let's start with the first few practical steps to get started:

1) Email Connie your first name and email address to register on her **"Together Let's Start A Village"** list. [connie@helpfromheaven.net]
2) Print (copy and paste) the one page description found on Connie's *"Messages From Heaven"* Facebook "ABOUT" page, and offer it to those who may be in alignment with this intentional way of living - living in a self-sustaining community that supports spiritual growth. Invite them to join with us.
3) Consider a monthly "meeting of the minds". I will ask Connie to schedule a group phone call. As you bring your active energy into this desire, in the form of thought, conversation and other action, my support will come into it. My power will begin to infuse into your desire for this and I will make it grow.

Jesus

Message from Heaven #131

Begin thinking of what it would be like living in such a community. Begin to imagine it. What would it be like to live amongst true friends? Friends who are capable of being kind, loving and caring to all; who think of the needs of others as much as themselves; who think of my desires; desires for freedom to live a balanced life, a healthy life, a non-poisonous life, a happier life; a more fulfilling life; a life filled with a joy you know not of yet; the joy of our Father; a comfort that surpasses all understanding that is within you constantly; trusting our Father to take care of everything; worry no more, nor fear or despair; knowing we are not separate – understanding this in your direct experience; supporting each other through times of healing; knowing you are never alone; waking up each day excited to begin it; filled with wonder and a happiness beyond the physical; working for something that has real meaning. A healed heart is what will bring this into fruition. Let me help you help yourself. I am here for all of you always. Make this a priority. Imagine this. Desire this.
Jesus

Message from Heaven #132

Many want to change their lives completely. Many are reaching a time of exasperation. Some of you are ready to just give up on life. Yet, you can't. You are not suicidal, but you simply do not want to continue living like this, feeling more and more daunted and depressed. There is little meaning in your life. There is little joy. There is little fulfillment. As a result, there is lack in your life; a lack of life energy in everything. You feel unsupported. Remember that feeling life energy – love, passion, joy - brings more of it.

I'd like to ask you to imagine as you used to when you were a child. Do this just a few times a day; just for a few minutes. When you do this, do it for my wishes, for my desires which I have expressed - a new way of life. See yourself and the whole world in love with life, in need of nothing, happy and free. I cannot live your lives for you. You have to be a part of creating your life and world. Only leave the 'how' of it up to God. Simply day dream about it. Feel it fully – living in a loving world, in harmony and joy and loving

yourselves and your lives. Put your attention on your inner feelings and how others are feeling inside. See yourselves happy, joyful and free. God will coordinate events that follow this. Leave solutions out of it. Leave the how to God. Just day dream about it.
Jesus

Message from Heaven #133

Some of you are feeling some frustration. You say you've been feeling that. I say you haven't – not like that. Enhance your ability to create like me. Feel like me. Feel loving, trusting, worry free. Feel joyful and grateful and humble. Feel in a place of surrendering to our Father with each experience, each moment. This can be very simple. The mind wants to create obstacles, but you do not have to believe in them. You can honor them and let them be without following them with your feelings. You can do this.

Day dreaming in this way a few minutes, a few times a day will quickly change the unconscious pattern you've been absorbed in. Your mind will say this is not good enough. Let it be, but do not unconsciously follow it with negative feelings or inaction. Know your mind's thoughts are problematic. That is its nature – to figure out solutions to the problems it creates. Simply honor that, accept that. Do not resist this and know it is not truth. Let your mind think as it thinks right now. Put your attention on feeling these feelings – a few minutes, a few times a day. This alone will effectively redirect the trend you're on.
Jesus

Message from Heaven #134

I would like to increase your power for you now. I would like to strengthen your ability to be more like me. This means being more aware that our Father is fully within you. You can induce the awakening of your soul's love immediately with an intention; an intention given in the right way – with devotion.

Tell God that your life is for Him. Tell Him you know this. If you do not feel you know this fully, that does not matter. It is the given intention of

your devotion that is needed. God takes it from there. Create a profound change in one minute; the biggest change of your lifetime. Consciously give your life to God. He has been waiting for this time. Just tell Him you want Him to take over your life. Tell Him you are willing to allow that; that you are ready for this and you desire this. There is a readiness within your consciousness now from reading my words that has not been there before. Trust me please. Just do it genuinely. I am communicating these words because you are ready for more of my power to come into your lives and world. I bring simplicity to everything. Remember this. It does not have to be complicated or challenging. My way is with simplicity. Give our Father this moment of intention today. Create a transformation that will come from it.
Jesus

Message from Heaven #135

I am now going to present something new to you; an idea. Let's connect 50 people that register on the **Together Let's Start a Village** list. Once there are 50 people with the same desire for creating and living in an intentional community such as this, let's begin the process for its creation. Your preferred choices will be up to you.

1) Your ideal location would be in the northern most top one-third of the United States or above. What country? What area? You can list a few options.
2) What is needed in this community to make it a self-sustaining community? This should include only those ways which do not poison yourselves or the earth:
   a) Power/electricity
   b) Water
   c) Food – sources/production
   d) Housing structures
   e) A healing facility

d) Rooms for learning and connecting a community of 50 that allows for growth to 300.
e) A dining area large enough for the community
f) What other buildings, rooms, stores or services would you like to have available?
g) Bring your resources together. Remember the story of the fishes and loaves of bread? Do not think about how little you may have. When you gather all resources, in harmony and unison, give them to me. Surrender what you have to me and I am the one who will multiply what you have into what you need. Remember not to limit me.
h) Then begin with a property in a desirable setting for my first community.
i) Begin to grow your own food in a healthy way. Have underground water available; bring your love into it – your new home environment. Expect it to be beautiful. Design it to your liking. Bring your creativity into it. Enjoy the process. Enjoy the journey of creating it. The logistics of everything will grow together daily. Anything you need along the way, get together as one and give it to me. We will create it together.

Jesus

Message from Heaven #136

I want you to know that you are creators. Understanding this intellectually is of little value. When you begin to experience this – when you begin to truly realize that you are not limited, that you are intended to experience the power of Divine love, a power that you do not control, but that you allow to take over your life and world, you are beginning to develop Christ consciousness; my level of awareness. This is when grace enters your life.

Struggle and effort begins to dissolve. A power overcomes you and you notice this. You witness this. This is the awakening of your soul's love. It is the awakening of our Father within you. It is something you know is not coming from you, but from something within you. You have reached a higher level of awareness now. From here, life becomes very different. Ego simply begins to dissolve.

Challenging experiences are not seen in the same way as before. Your perception starts to shift. It is my light - our Father's light - that begins to expand within your consciousness. This changes everything spontaneously. Your heart is not the same. It is opening wider now – literally. More light is shining through it. It is a letting go of the separate you as unity consciousness begins to develop.

As time goes by, so long as you do not restrict it, God's love and power begins to create your life for you. Experiencing the divine begins to redefine you. This means more love energy. Conscious surrendering to our Father is needed now more than ever.

The ego will want to find fault more than before. Ego will put up a fight for control. It, your mind's perception, which is just an illusion that you believe in, will grow more fearful. It wants to survive, not vanish. So, a conscious awareness - intentional awareness of your fear is of great value. In time, it will not be there anymore. But, this is a transition new to you and it requires some experience to become proficient with trusting in this power.

You do not intellectually understand it and the mind feels powerless to control as much as before so it will want to become stronger. A conscious awareness of your fearful thoughts and feelings are needed; otherwise they will control you. And, fearful thoughts and feelings take you away from God when you are unaware of them. It is awareness now that is your savior – my awareness – Christ consciousness. You want to allow it – your fear to be there. Resisting it will not make it weaker. It is the opposite.

Many of you have begun this initial process. Many are near reaching the initial awakening of my love and power. You need to know how to handle your fear now more than before. Your ego's fear will become more clever. It wants to bring your awareness back down to it. So, conscious awareness of your fearful feelings – without resisting them, is needed. Now is a time to watch yourself. Literally watch yourself as if you were me, watching you lovingly and adoringly. This is what brings consciousness into your direct experience.

There is no judgment involved. Just witness what is happening within your consciousness and physical body. Pretend you are me watching you. This is the only thing you need do to allow it. I will do the rest to continue your progress of allowing more fear to dissolve and more love to expand.
Jesus

Falling in Love with Your Life

Message from Heaven #137

MAKING THE TRANSITION from ego-awareness to God-awareness is a completely different way of living. Every belief you have gets challenged. Your true self, who has no fear, perceives every minute detail of every circumstance differently. Your perception right now comes from your ego. And right now, you perceive fearfully. You believe in a separate existence. You do not yet know that we are all one and not separate from God at all. You do not yet experience divine love, which is entirely different from "human" love – the loving of one separate human being from another.

Your perception is filled with the core fear of existing separately from God. This distorts everything else - how you see yourself, others and the world. You believe that you, as well as all others, are separate and not good enough; incomplete, not whole; not fully lovable. This creates the dysfunctional world in which you live. Lack, limitations and problems are created because you believe in the ego's perception, which created them. What you believe creates your physical manifestations – every single one of them. If you perceive everyone and everything as separate from God, separate from wholeness, incomplete and defective, this is what you create in the physical.

The only thing you need ever do, is to expand your awareness of knowing the truth. Your soul already knows the truth. But, you still operate from your ego's awareness right now. You try to control and create your physical experience from the level of your ego's awareness. The only thing you ever have control over is your own perception; your own awareness.

Trying to fix and repair a broken band aid will not fix the symptom of the problem. Trying to fix the symptom will also not solve what created the problem. Another problem follows another problem ongoing. You are stuck in trying to fix problems, not on what creates them. What is needed to get out of this ignorance is to understand that it is your beliefs that create everything in your physical life. And if you believe you are separate from God, wholeness, perfection, pure love, you create the opposite of this – limitations, dysfunctions and problems, which brings ongoing pain and suffering.

Expanding your awareness means expanding the growth of your soul, the answer to all problems. Simply put, your soul's awareness is more dormant than your ego's right now. Your ego's perception needs to grow out of itself in order for your soul's awareness to take over. This is a transition from ignorance to truth, from fear to love, from judgment to compassion and forgiveness, from sin to sinless, from evil to good.

Put attention on your awareness – your perception, not your problems. Your goal is to develop my perception – Christ consciousness. Know that if you believe this is not possible or that it is too good for you, you will remain in your present state of limitation and dysfunction. This means staying in one form of trial and tribulation to another; involved in another 'problem' to be resolved again and again.

You will never fix the source of problems with the level of consciousness that created them. Trying to do so keeps you unconsciously stuck in re-creating them. Focus on your level of consciousness. It is your increased consciousness that effortlessly dissolves them. When your consciousness becomes more like mine, problems disappear on their own. Your consciousness needs to grow. This means your heart's love; your soul. Please practice the *Hope Technique* and the *Heart Technique* daily.
Jesus

Message from Heaven #138
Can you understand more now that growing up spiritually is needed to be like me? Do not put me in a separate box from you. I am not any better than you. Your mind will tell you otherwise, just do not believe in it. You need the willingness to expand your mind's beliefs to being more in alignment with mine. Do not believe you cannot be like me. This is your destiny.

Every single one of you will reach it. But, when you do is up to you. Let go of thinking in a box – a box that you've been taught is truth. Remember that your elders are learning how to grow spiritually too. You need the willingness to grow and to think more like me to become more of who you really are. The true you knows everything as I do. You are as worthy of this awareness as I am. Remind yourself of this please.
Jesus

Message from Heaven #139
I'd like to talk about our Father some more. I want you to better understand Him. That being said, know you will never understand our Father without the experience of Him. Do not forget this so you do not stay stuck in your head. Intellectual knowledge will never get you in love with Him.

I'd like to explain how it all gets started – a love affair with God. It begins with realizing that nothing in the physical world will ever fulfill you. When you realize this, you are ready to grow spiritually at a much more rapid pace. You begin to seek Him.

This is usually when you are on your knees, so broken, you've given up on your wants; your own desires. If you want something more from the physical world, you do not want God enough to draw Him close to you. You must want God to develop within you. Your desire is needed to create this awakening.

Falling in love with God is an experience that needs cultivating. Since you only know life from the physical world, you do not yet know Him. You can intentionally get to know Him by intentionally wanting Him. Your wanting Him is needed to become Him. Until you want God fully, your direct experience of Him will be limited.

I was born as all of you were. But, I mastered forgiveness quickly. I learned not to resist evil well. Evil is fear. I learned how to forgive it – fear. I honored it. I allowed it to be. I did not try to resist it, ignore it or pretend it wasn't there. I faced it. I felt it and I accepted it being there. You already know this is doing the *HOPE Technique*.

The only thing standing in your way from uniting with our Father is your fear. You understand this more now. But, what are you doing? The same thing as always? Hiding from your misery? Going about your day pretending it's not there? Distracting yourself from it with one activity to the next? Anyone that does not know our Father is living in misery, whether you acknowledge this or not. Most are so used to it you just don't know anything else.

I have given you a way to freedom quickly. Yet, you are ignoring that. Stay dormant in your darkness no more. Have courage and face what is there. Why wait until later to realize our Father?

Falling in love with God is a process; the most beautiful, magnificent experience imaginable. The more you love Him, the more you attract Him. The initial awakening of falling in love with God comes when you have nothing else to fight for; nothing else to strive for. You give up. This is the moment I am waiting for. This is when you can utilize me more fully. This is when you allow me to take over and your heart opens just a little for the first time. This is when you begin to fall in love with God. Now we are together like never before. We are on the journey together as one. You are with me in your heart, just a little. That's all it takes.

Can you understand that when this occurs, you are not the same person anymore? You change overnight. You now consciously want God from your heart. When you reach this point in your life, this is what you do next to intentionally fall in love with our Father:

- Talk to Him. Talk with Him from your heart. Tell Him how you are feeling, what you need His help with and for all that you are grateful to Him. Talk to Him frequently.
- Have the thought throughout the day that you want to please Him; that you want to serve Him; that you want to make Him proud of you and all you do. Live for Him, not for yourself.
- Give what you have to help others. Give your money, possessions, time, kindness, love. Each day give some of what you have to help His children.
- Acknowledge to yourself and to Him that He is your provider of everything good.
- Tell Him you are thankful that He brought you to me.
- Be loving and kind to all life; people, animals and the earth.

- Say nothing that is false.
- Speak without negativity.
- Live abundantly in your thinking, not frugally.
- When you go to sleep at night, make our Father the last thing you think about.
- Enjoy your time. Change your life if needed to enjoy your time.
- Tell Him you want Him frequently.
- Read books that make you feel more open hearted and connected to God and that inspire you to feel more loving.
- Connect with others regularly who are also interested in developing their soul's awareness.
- Spend more time in nature.
- Ask me and Babaji for our personal help and support.

Jesus

Message from Heaven #140

Make amends to yourself from the past. It is always your own guilt that leads to all other forms of painful feelings. I'd like to expand your thinking about yourself. Many of you think you are not good enough for God. Many of you think you are not good enough for me. You have a concept of God that is distorted. You've been taught that you need to sacrifice yourself for Him; sex, money, comfort, companionship, peace, fun, happiness and joy. Many of you have been taught that the more you suffer or struggle, the more you are deserving of God's love.

Even if you consciously tell yourself you know this is not true, there is something deep within you that hangs onto these beliefs. They are imbedded in you. This is a result of an inner guilt that is connected to your love for God. There is something inside of you that knows you chose to forget Him.

There is also a deeply imbedded belief within you that believes suffering is the way to forgiveness from God; that if you suffer enough, He will forgive you of your wrongs. This creates an underlying fear of yourself – of your Higher Self, which **is** God. God will emerge fully through each of you when you are willing to forgive yourself from what is not even real to begin with.

Your perception has lost awareness of God, but you have never, nor could ever lose God. He is what keeps you living each moment. He is Life itself before all form. Who keeps your heart beating? What keeps you breathing? How does the sun keep shining? How are the flowers blooming? It is our Father – Life Energy. You are never without It.

If you simply remind yourself daily that God is fully within you already and that there is nothing to forgive in the first place, this will help you open up to loving God more and fearing Him less. This includes your Higher Self. This will help you forgive your own guilt. Know that I love you regardless of what you think you have done wrong. Know that in my world, there is no such thing. Just remind yourself of this.
Jesus

Message from Heaven #141

Do you want to know more about me? You can read about me or you can experience me. Which would you prefer? There is so much reading about me and too little of experiencing me. I am a level of consciousness. God brought me to earth to develop His state of awareness. This means a fully loving state. This means without fear. All of you are here for the same purpose; to develop your hearts to fullness. When you accomplish this, you have my level of consciousness; God consciousness.

The more you develop my level of consciousness, the more we become as one; the more you experience my heart. The joy and fulfillment, for which you are all searching, will only come from experiencing God consciousness. The more you develop me, the happier and more peaceful you become. There is an inner love and joy that you are all seeking, but many of you do not seek beyond your physical world. You are clinging to something in the physical world to seek for that which is not physical. There is no situation, no person or thing that will ever satisfy or fulfill you.

That emptiness inside, that hollow feeling of something missing, is the lack of my love. It is waiting to be experienced through you. This is what you are searching for but you do not know where to find. I want you to want me and my level of consciousness. But, you are so busy in activity, you are unable to connect to me. You cannot experience me. You cannot know me.

I understand it is becoming increasingly challenging to be in stillness for many of you. Your minds are so busy with so many thoughts that when you start to slow down it feels uncomfortable. Your suppressed, buried feelings come to the surface of your awareness then. It seems more comfortable to continue to ignore them. You do not want to feel them. You have been doing this a very long time; ignoring what's in your heart – the pain and fear.

It is a part of you right now. The only way to be rid of it is to heal it. This means to face it and feel it. Freedom is on the other side. It is a freedom you will all reach in time. Any ongoing agony you continue to live with will not go away until your full awareness is given to it.

What is the alternative? Insanity; complete and utter insanity. Many of you are more than half way there. You are near the end of having a choice in the matter. When there is no way of pulling yourself out of being stuck, God will have to do it for you, all Himself. This means a hard wake up call for you. It is only so you can continue to grow. Our Father will not leave you lost in the dark forever. He loves you.

Are you going to join with me or not? I have personally asked you to join me. Sit with my invitation for a few minutes in silence. Feel your heart. Where is it leaning? Toward my community that is intended for you? There is a higher quality of life waiting for you there. A quality of living that you do not yet know exists. You cannot continue living solo much longer. It simply will not be supported anymore. Our Father wants you to grow. He wants to experience more through you.

Jesus

Message from Heaven #142

You are here to enjoy living in a physical world; to enjoy the fruits it has to offer. Experiencing what you love doing is why you are all here. But, when there is fear in your perception that you are missing something, 'need' becomes a part of your experience. The more you feel in a state of need, the more you fear.

As a result, you will experience more need – more lack of abundance. This infuses into every aspect of your life. Remember that you create what you believe. Needing anything but God's love is actually self-damaging.

Many of you think that it is you who supplies yourself with whatever you need. This way of thinking is incorrect. Acknowledgment of your true Source is greatly needed. By not recognizing that our Father is the Supplier of all your needs and everything good in your life, keeps you in more suffering than you know. It keeps you in lack of more goodness. It keeps you in worry, fear and resentment. A life-changing transformation occurs when you consciously acknowledge that you can create nothing without our Father, for He is the Supplier of all. I'd like to explain why.

What you judge from your experiences become your beliefs. Your beliefs become your own version of reality. There is great creative power behind these beliefs. So, when you think you are the creator, you leave God out of your consciousness. This is when you lose His power to create more good. When you fail to acknowledge Him as the Source of all, you lose the benefit of His loving power for the creation of loving and joyful experiences. This results in a meaningless life and one with effort.

Simply put, your love for God is greatly minimized when you do not acknowledge Him for all that you receive. So, there is literally less love in your hearts. It is His love that creates everything good. Increase your love for God. This will automatically bring more love and abundance into your experiences.
Jesus

Message from Heaven #143

When you begin to awaken your heart just a little, you begin to develop a more personal relationship with me. I want you to know what this means. There is a difference between honoring me in your mind and surrendering your heart to me. It is the conscious surrendering of your life to me that sparks the initial awakening in your heart. It is the bridge, the connector to you and the Creator, our Father.

Many of you think that because you honor me and my teachings, this has already been accomplished. Many of you think you have surrendered your lives to me, but you haven't; not yet. You can tell me you want this, but if you follow this intention while still holding onto your same judgments, it is not real. A level of compassion and non-judgment must first be developed. This is a gray area for many. Not understanding what this means can be an obstacle. So, I would like to clarify this.

If you think you are better than anyone because of your beliefs, you are not there yet. If you think you are higher or closer to God due to your specific beliefs, you are not there yet. You are still in the mind set of being God and not in a true place of surrender to God. This surrender, the surrender of your love to all, is what is needed to initially open your heart and begin the process of developing Christ consciousness.

This is when your life begins to change in a whole new way. We unite through your heart, not your mind. Remember that all of your beliefs come from your mind but it is your heart you want to connect with. This requires a surrendering of your present beliefs. A moment of grace, a feeling of more freedom and ease comes into your consciousness when this happens. It is unmistakable. You will know it when it happens. Reading my *Messages from Heaven* will induce this awakening and continue to enliven it. Please connect with me further by reading my messages.
Jesus

Message from Heaven #144

I am bringing each of you a level of love that is going to change your world; the whole earth. I am going to restore your lives and your world. It has already begun to happen. These messages of mine are the beginning of this healing taking place. You are ready for this. Our Father is ready for this. I am going to be open and honest with you as always, but it is something many of you may not want to hear. You can ignore it or you can benefit from it. This is your own choice to make. I am not asking Connie to share my messages to make you falsely feel rosy in your ignorance. I am sharing my messages to save the world.

Many of you will drift away and that is okay. The ones that remain in a place of openness to my messages will create a new life on earth. Know this will be the minority, not the majority. The people who followed me as Jesus Christ on earth were of the few. There are not limitations as a result of this. That is the ego's fearful thinking, not truth. Just know this. There is no lack of power in my desires.

I would like you to understand that there is a war coming to earth. It is unstoppable. Father has allowed it. In fact, He is supporting it. You will not wake up without it. When you hear the government asking for a new number for each of you, this is the formation of this world war. The creation of this war will not be a slow progression. It will begin without notice soon after. At this time, if you are not two-thirds of the way north in the United States, you will be among the forgotten. This means the people who have chosen to forget me. This means my love. They have chosen a different route to grow toward me.

You will be among the healers and rebuilders. You will be in my safety. Do not forget this. I will bring you what you need to create freedom for all once again. I'd like to ask you to consider what this means so you have a more realistic view. Ignorance is always a chosen condition. Ignorance will not save you.

You will need to make some changes to follow me and you may not want to make them. Know that your decisions are based on how your lives are now. Know that they will be very different in a world war. You would be happy then to change your location and way of living to not be a part of that chaos. Yet, you will not have the freedom or ability to make these changes then. Now is the time to get started with the creation of my communities for each of you. Fear not. Fear accomplishes nothing helpful. Trust in me. This is all you need.
Jesus

Message from Heaven #145

Being a follower of ignorance is a dangerous trap. It is subtle – ignorance. It always accompanies unconsciousness. Unconsciousness is without conscious awareness. It seems to happen without choice, but this is not true. There are so many opportunities that you choose to ignore. It is intentional avoidance behavior. Your fear drives this. It is what creates your dysfunctional world. It is a self-chosen role of ignorance. It seems to make the fear go away, but it actually creates more of it.

If you were to simply face the fear when it comes to your awareness, you would annihilate it. Your awareness would resolve it automatically. Those who live in ignorance, ignoring the truth, create all forms of havoc. If you faced it with grace - with honesty and trust, it simply would not be there anymore. What do you see in the world that you are not in agreement with in your heart? What feels not right? What feels not in alignment with me and my teachings?

The suffering of many pass through your consciousness each day. It is your ignoring it that created it in the first place. Your fear creates as much as your love. Know that whatever is in your consciousness, you create. And if there is fear there, it creates pain and suffering in various ways. The pain is there to let you know something isn't right. It is divine guidance, yet you continually strive to ignore it. A cycle of sickness and dysfunction from one form to the next becomes a part of your lives and world.

I conquered the world by facing all fear. In a short time, I realized it wasn't real to begin with. This is when you become God – a Son or Daughter of God. It is full realization of truth. If you asked yourself just once a day, *"What am I ignoring that is not God's way – that is not loving"*? You would quickly turn around the ignorance you are in. This would put an end to all suffering. All forms of discord would not be supported anymore. You have the power to do this. You are not the sheep you pretend to be.

Bring love into this world. I cannot do this for you without you. It is your world that you live in. You have to be the ones to create it. Yet, know I will help you if you are willing. We can do more together than you know. It is necessary for you to be alignment with me. It is necessary to be in alignment with being loving. Keeping your love in a box between you and your own family and circle of friends will not wake up this world. You have to develop your hearts beyond that.

How can you help someone that is in a state of suffering or struggle? What can you do? Are you too busy in your own separate world to care? You do know where they are. They are everywhere. You are supporting it by doing nothing. This is a self-chosen role. I want all of my children to be happy and free and fully aware of me. I want us as one again in your world, not only the spiritual realm. Do not wait until you are there to care. It does not work that way. You first have to create it in your physical world.

Be followers of an unconscious life no more. Start facing your fear to get out of it. Ask yourself that question please, daily. Then do something about it.
Jesus

Message from Heaven #146

To gain more grace, ask for it every day. Let God know you want Him for your every need. With enough grace, you need nothing else, not even food or water. Spiritual energy, this non-physical energy, is your only true Life Force. It is the only thing you ever truly need. It is your eternal self; it is also your Father. It is invisible to the human eye, for it contains no physical matter. Yet, it is there. It supplies all life.

There is much more spiritual power available to you than you realize. You simply have not learned how to receive it yet. But, you will. Your mind has to accept it first to enable it to flow through you more fully. Your mind is a stumbling block to this. You are naturally meant to have my amount of Life Force within you. As it grows from within, you need less physical resources. You will begin to rely solely on our Father's power as you let go of your need to control your physical world. You are intended to experience the physical existence, but without being in need of it for anything.

You do not yet know this level of existence but, you will. I'd like to expand your consciousness so you can begin to allow more of your Life Force to flow through you. What blocks it from expanding is your limited thinking. Remember that your beliefs create your reality. So, if you cannot grow your mind's beliefs, you will remain as limited as they are.

How do you think I supplied what I did from nothing? What about the bread and wine? What about the blind man's eyes? And the sick and the dead brought back to life again? It is natural to have domain over the physical, not the other way around.

Try to imagine a life without limitations. What would you have it be like? What would you do? Who would you be experiencing through? The true you is not only physical. You do have full domain over your body and world. You have only forgotten this. And, as always, what you believe is what you create. Start thinking beyond your present reality as you know it. Imagine living in a world where you can create what you experience. Unlimited thinking creates unlimited living. Grow beyond your mind's present beliefs.
Jesus

Message from Heaven #147

There is a way to develop the power of God within you, toward the creation of your desires. When your desires involve the love for all, there is no limitation to what you can create. Until you are God-realized, consciously surrender each moment to Him. When you have surrendered the desire to control your life and your world and you become one with Him in your awareness, you will then have my ability available to create.

Surrendering to each moment requires continuous conscious awareness. This means the desire to allow God to operate your life and everything else. Without your conscious desire to let Him take it over, He will not. This means you will continue to coordinate your life. And, until you are free of fear and God-realized, you will bring struggle and limitation into whatever you create.

Your lives are intended to be of complete and total freedom from suffering, struggle, limitation, sickness and lack. All of these dysfunctions occur because you are trying to govern your life and your world. When you have grown spiritually to the point that you surrender your fearful thinking, fearful feelings will be no more. That is when you gain the full power of God to create your life. This is freedom. This is salvation. This is the attainment of God-consciousness.

Intentional surrender of every minute weeds out your fear more effectively than anything else. Simply put, you begin a new habit. This will lead to dissolving all problems in the world. Instead of trying to fix them yourself, you allow God to do it for you by simply wanting Him to. It is truly easy. You just need to create a new habit of surrendering.

Remember though, the ego does not want this to be. The ego losing itself means its death. It is a force, it is an influence. And, you unconsciously continue to feed it. You do this unknowingly and automatically. You do not know any other way. This is because you have forgotten God. It is a dysfunctional, delusional world you live in because of this.

Bring awareness into it. When you notice you are feeling less than loving and not in a place of trust, ease and grace – inner peace – a feeling of resisting - surrender that moment to God. Consciously say, *"God, please take this; I give it to you now; I want to follow your lead instead of my own"*. Doing this will create a new trend. You will change your lives and world. You are intentionally wanting to trust God instead of your ego self. This is the world-changing moment I am waiting for with each of you.

This is when you are allowing me to enter your life and create it for you. This is a completely different way of living. It will bring you the peace, freedom, love and the power of God. This message is about surrender – surrendering your fearful thinking and beliefs - to God's loving guidance and direction. It is not doing more, it is doing less. This is needed to bring God into it.

Ego wants to "do". Ego wants to control. Ego wants to believe it has the power. It strives to have more control and power in any way it can. And notice, it always uses fear to do this. It is your fear and you are controlled by it right now. You cannot fight this tendency within you. What you need to do is bring awareness of it into your consciousness. Then simply surrender it to God when you notice this *'resistance'* type of energy within you. This is all you need do to create a new trend rather than to continue following it in ignorance.

Jesus

Message from Heaven #148

Begin to create a new life in your head. Use your imagination. As long as your desires are in alignment with loving to all, there is nothing you cannot create. You have the capacity to be a creator like me. We were born the same; in a human form. I was also a man. The only difference is that I brought forth God's love fully through my physical form. That is what makes me seem different than you.

I developed my consciousness fully by surrendering all of my fears to our Father. I consciously gave them all to Him. This simple intention of giving Him your fears to take care of for you, which includes any perceived problem imaginable, will transition your thinking to being more as you truly are – God unlimited. All limitations of any kind are always a result of incorrect thinking. Yet, if you believe your thoughts are truth, they are truth for you.

Transition your thinking to being more in alignment with truth. You can naturally grow out of them. This means you let go of trying to control each and every present moment. This means surrendering each present moment to our Father. This transition can happen quickly. It will lead to gaining the power of love; the perfection of love; the peace of love; the joy of love. Grace. This brings the grace of God through you.

If you believe you are God before you are free of all fear, it is your ego's fear that takes over. If you surrender to God until you are free of all fear, you will become free of fear and develop God within you.

God realization is the believing in no fear and being fully loving. So, while you presently have fear, you want to strengthen your love and reduce your fear. **You do this by cultivating your love for God and surrendering your fears to Him.** This transitions your thinking from fear to love. This transitions your consciousness from fear to love. This transitions your fearful lives to fearless lives. This leads to having no limitations, no dysfunctions. This leads to God consciousness – the knowing that you already *are* God. This leads to enlightenment on earth for all.

Jesus

Stilling the Mind's Thoughts

Message from Heaven #149

As I have mentioned, many are starting to feel a deeper yearning, an inner longing for something more and it is your soul calling you to awaken. It is our Father's love. It is usually a feeling that passes through you very quickly and you give it little attention. You are too distracted in busyness. Busyness in action and busyness in your mind. You are not with stillness enough to connect with it. Remember that the presence of God is in pure stillness. To connect with It, become more in tune with It. The more often you connect with It, the more of your Life Force enlivens within you. I have described the feeling that accompanies this as much as words can convey. It is an aliveness, a love and comfort that is so beautiful it is unimaginable. It is our Father. It is our true home.

This message is going to discuss something vitally important that enables you to connect with our Father's energy directly. It is about meditation. I will give you my definition of meditation, for there are many varying methods. It is a practice that intentionally stills the mind's thoughts.

I gave Mette (Connie's friend) the *Heart Technique* practice to teach to others. The first part of the *Heart Technique* is a specific meditation that stills the mind's thoughts. This part is crucial for the rest of the *Heart Technique* to be effective – because if you cannot slow down your thinking, you can accomplish little else.

A mantra meditation should remain easy and effortless – without input of focus or concentration. It is most important to learn this properly. Otherwise, you will not receive the full benefits from this practice.

Personalized instruction and follow-up from an experienced meditation teacher is vital for the success of this program.

I would like to talk to you more about why it is essential to practice a meditation that uses my mantra – the sound of creation: "I AM". The correct application of this sound creates a subtle energy reverberation throughout your nervous system. It attracts the presence of God to awaken within you.

With the daily practice of this meditation, your body's energy gradually changes to be more in alignment with the energy of God; His presence. It is the presence of His peace that passes all understanding that you have heard about. Simply put, connecting daily with this stillness energy awakens your soul. Reducing your mind's thoughts is necessary to accomplish this. You cannot merge with God's loving, peaceful power if your thoughts are too busy. This is what I'd like to discuss with you further.

It is going to be very challenging for you to alter the quality of energy in your consciousness and body **if** you do not practice an effective meditation daily. There is a momentum of busy, scattered and stressful energy within most of you. You cannot turn this cycle around to a calmer, more peaceful place without practicing a daily meditation such as this. Your minds are simply in a mode of busyness; of unconsciousness. Expanding your consciousness is necessary to become more in alignment with the state of consciousness of enlightenment.

For those of you who already practice a mantra meditation, I would like to ask you to change your mantra to "I AM". It is ready to be practiced now by all. If you are used to your own mantra, you may not want to change it. Your nervous system is already integrated with the sound effect of your own mantra and it is comfortably familiar to you. There is nothing wrong with other mantras, but I would like to have all of you using this same mantra. I will explain why.

"I AM" is the sound of creation. There is no other sound that influences your energy more in alignment with God's loving energy than this. Mantras influence the energy in your body and the mantra, "I AM", is going to help you enhance the world's collective consciousness much more effectively. You are ready to unify more in this way. It is time to merge your consciousness with the presence of God. The more of you who use this

mantra, the more support and influence you contribute to each other's spiritual growth. Remember the saying that two people praying together is stronger than one? It is like this. Two lights are brighter than one. Shine your lights together, please. Shine in harmony and unison with each other. Become a more effective, collective source as one light calling our Father in stillness.
Jesus

Message from Heaven #150

When you are sleeping there is something that happens in your consciousness. Right now, this can only happen in your sleep. I'd like to talk about this with you. It will help you understand more about how your consciousness works.

Your consciousness is much more open when you are sleeping. This is because your mind's thoughts are less in control. Consciousness is hard for the mind to fully understand; in fact it is impossible. Consciousness is not something physical. You do not experience it from within the five physical senses. Remember that the mind can only identify through the experience of the five physical senses. If you cannot touch, hear, taste, smell or see it, the mind cannot fully comprehend it.

Your consciousness is your awareness. It could also be called your perception; how you perceive everything. It is what you perceive. When you are awake, your mind's beliefs taint your perception.

Your present beliefs limit your awareness greatly. When you are awake, your perception is dominated by the thoughts that you believe in. When you believe in fear, the fear distorts how you perceive every moment. I have explained that with the underlying core belief that you exist as separate from your Creator and all else, you perceive everything skewed, with separation and fear. This is a fearful belief. Right now, most of you on earth believe you are separate from God, me, each other and all. As a result, you have an underlying feeling that something is missing, that you are incomplete and that you are not good enough. This is where your consciousness is presently at.

When you are sleeping, the fear you believe in is still in your consciousness, but you are not aware of it. This creates a window of opportunity to become more aware of God; simply because fear is not controlling your thinking.

I would like to share a powerful method of intentionally expanding your consciousness while you are sleeping. Many of you will not want to put in this effort. So, this is for the few of you who do. In time, it will require no effort, as it will occur spontaneously. But, this requires a letting go of being the one in control of your thoughts, and that, you are simply not accustomed. So, although it may seem as though some effort is required at first, know this is your natural way of utilizing your mind, without it trying to control everything. This is a practice of surrendering while you are sleeping.

Before you go to sleep at night; after the lights are out and you are more relaxed, do this:

Feel love. Feel your love for me. You want to put your gentle attention on your physical heart while you are doing this. Place your attention to your heart's location. Have the intention of feeling **its** loving energy extending toward me. Now imagine I am feeling it, that I notice it, and that you've got my full attention from it. You are drawing my attention to you directly. You are now connecting with **my** awareness of your heart's loving energy.

Know that I am fully loving you for doing this. I am giving you back my powerful, loving and adoring attention. I am never not loving and adoring you fully, but I want you to bring your awareness of **my awareness** into your consciousness for a few minutes before you go to sleep. This will bring more of my consciousness into your consciousness while you sleep. Simply put, a few moments before you sleep, put your attention of feeling your love for me and my love for you.
Jesus

Message from Heaven #151

There is another way to still the mind's thoughts. Intentionally think of me throughout your day. It is simple, yet challenging to maintain because your thoughts are so habitual right now. You have developed a momentum of thinking in a scattered way – one thought after the other randomly, without having any intention behind them. Basically, your thoughts are in a momentum on automatic. You have little control over them. Your thoughts actually control you rather than you directing them. This is what makes up the scattered, unconscious, chaotic and unhealthy world you live in.

You have lost domain over your lives and world. The force behind your thoughts is fearful energy. And it is this fearful energy that drives you and everything you do. Most everyone lives in this state of unconsciousness; unknowingly allowing your fear to control you. Most of your thoughts are fearful. You go from one to the next habitually and automatically and it has become 'normal' to you. You do not even recognize all that you have lost. You have lost your power. You have lost your true self. You have lost your awareness of God.

You live in worry and fear, so you create more fearful experiences – sickness, dysfunctions, chaos, abuse, violence, poverty, a meaningless life with various forms of pain and suffering. Our Father did not create this. You did through the forgetting of Him. **You** have the power to create what is in **your** consciousness. You have all the power as I have. But, you have lost the ability to know how to use it.

This is because your minds go from one negative, fear-based thought to another all day long. Your minds have been in this cycle for so long, it seems normal to you now. Staying in this cycle will lead to destroying yourselves. Less fearful thinking is needed to change this unconscious pattern from continuing.

Without your desire to improve the quality of your thoughts, you will not. This will create a certain outcome. Allow me to come into your thinking. Intentionally think of me being with you. Have your attention, your awareness, on me being with you throughout your day. Also, know I am loving you. Do realize that this alone will turn your world around. It will if you are thinking of me; if you have me in your conscious awareness. You will be directly connecting with me intentionally. You will begin to have my influence in your thinking, feelings, behaviors and life. Then, I will create the healing, the balance, the reorganization of your life and world.

Jesus

Message from Heaven #152

Happiness comes automatically when your soul is growing. I have said this before. I am repeating it for a reason. I want you to understand this more. An inner feeling of emptiness occurs when you are in a place of spiritual stagnation; a meaningless life results. Your life becomes dull, empty and mundane and then you become numb. Many of you live in this state until you die. You think it is how life is. You work to survive until you die. You try to have some pleasurable experiences as often as possible, but these times are usually limited to a weekend off or a vacation, if you are fortunate enough to get that.

You are not thinking of how unnatural this is compared to how your lives are intended to be. You unconsciously go along with it. You have conformed to a way of living without God in it. When I say God, I mean Life Energy. This is loving, happiness energy; feeling joyful, relaxed, and completely fulfilled. This creates living in a state of gratitude. What most of you consider gratitude is nothing in comparison to the level of gratitude I am referring to.

If you do not have the desire for "more" – more of your natural state of experience, you will continue living a life of stagnation, without much meaning, and with trials and tribulations. I'd like to ask you to imagine more - more purpose and fulfillment; a meaningful life filled with genuine gratitude. This requires putting some energy into it; energy in the form of thinking, feeling and action. You need to recreate what you think about, what you feel and what you do.

Most of you have accepted an extremely reduced quality of life - one without God consciousness. What do you value most right now? You all value these qualities: love, joy, peace, usefulness, meaning, gratitude, happiness and fulfillment. What do you think will give you this? A nicer car or a bigger house? A higher status or social position? More friends or vacations? A soul mate? You often put your attention on these "things", these situations, and not on the experience behind them – love, peace, joy, happiness, fun, meaning, fulfillment, etc.

Right now, your mind decides what it believes will make you happy and fulfilled. That is based on your ego's beliefs – which will always believe in your fears and that you are separate from love. Happiness, wholeness and fulfillment are "out there somewhere". Such is the ego's perception. To believe otherwise is to bring death to the ego, which the ego always fights to avoid. Remember the ego always wants to keep you "striving and striving but never arriving".

Let God choose what will bring you happiness and fulfillment. This means to let go of trying to control and manipulate your life and all that is around you. You now do this to create what you believe will fulfill you. Let God take on this role. You will become directed in the flow of divine guidance. Transition from how you live each moment for what your ego wants, **to what you think God wants**.

It is only the wanting to do this that is needed to come into the flow of God's guidance, wisdom and power. You will begin to let go of trying to be God before you have developed Him within you. Most of you do this unknowingly. This is because your minds control your thinking, feelings and actions. Your minds have taken over your life and world. Your lives are literally an illusion because of this.

For most of you, life is like being actors on a stage; actors who have forgotten that the scene on the stage is only a temporary reality and not a 'true' one. Your physical reality (world) is created for your entertainment and meant to be enjoyed for a while. But, you have forgotten that the roles you play in your lives are not who you really are. It is a only a role you have chosen for a while.

When you desire to be aware of what God wants, you then begin to transform this illusory reality into true reality. You travel from illusion to truth. You may not intellectually understand this fully, but you will begin to experience it by having the conscious desire; the conscious intent to let go of what you think is needed, into what you think God wants.
Jesus

Message from Heaven #153
An Experience of a Higher State of Consciousness (#2): This experience happened several years after my previous "spiritual awakening experience" (shared in #128). This one occurred while I was sleeping. Some call this an "out of the body experience".

The only way I can word this, is that it was my "awareness" that woke up one night, during my sleep. (My body continued to sleep). My awareness, my pure existence, was coming from above my physical body, at about the height of the ceiling. I saw my body lying there sleeping. I immediately recognized how I felt completely free of physical pain, discomfort, limitation and the state of extreme fear and anxiety I was constantly in. I had been extremely ill from being severely mercury poisoned and with Lyme disease. Some doctors did not expect me to live and I was in a lot of physical pain and in constant fear of dying on a daily basis. Point being, I was in physical survival mode at this time. (I did fully recover five years later).

I saw my body and all of the room from the view of being at the level of the ceiling. The freedom I felt from not being in my physical body is simply beyond what words can describe. I felt extreme joy, relief, peace and complete freedom. I felt extreme love and was in bliss. I started to intentionally look around the room more in a state of awe and it was like I had x-ray vision. I saw all of the many atoms in the walls, on the floor, in the furniture, etc. I instantly knew these "things/objects" were actually alive. Living microscopic particles of living energy were in everything, everywhere; even in the air. Everything had these particles of living energy and they were actually moving; constantly flickering-fluttering and vibrating. They were little sparkles of white light, constantly moving. I remember thinking they looked like miniature sparkles of lightning bolts.

I instantly KNEW that these miniature particles of constantly moving, vibrating white light, was God. I just knew that it was "God energy". I was in extreme awe and fascinated with what I instantly realized. I thought to myself, *"oh my gosh, this is what they mean when they say that God is everywhere! I get it, I get it now! I totally understand! God is this "Life Energy" that is alive and everywhere and in and of everything"*! I was fascinated that I was capable of seeing this, what I now knew was always there, but could not normally see.

I had the thought of seeing my two dogs that were sleeping out in the living room. I, my awareness, was instantly in the living room, still viewing everything from the view of the ceiling. I looked around at everything in the living room; the furniture, my dogs. Everything in there was "alive", with these living, moving miniature particles that I knew was God Energy. I was in awe and pure freedom. I kept saying to myself, *"So, this is God, so this is what God is!"* It is a vast understatement to say that I felt an "enlightenment".

A thought spontaneously came to me that I wanted to stay in this state forever and never, ever go back into my physical body. That very second, my awareness was back in my body, as it was lying there sleeping. But, I did not feel the pain, discomfort or restriction of being in my body yet. I starting saying to myself that I had to remember "how I left my body like this. I have to remember, so when I wake up, I will not forget." It was the most absolute most important thing for me to remember how I did this.

The next thing I remember, I woke up in the morning as usual and in my normal state of awareness and in my normal state of physical pain and discomfort and in intense fear and panic again.

The contrast of this was so extreme and the loss was excruciatingly painful. I was already suicidal at this time, as I had been very ill and in a lot of pain for over a couple years. I was feeling hopeless that I was going to live through this, as I had seen many doctors and specialists already express that "I may not make it or end up with permanent nerve, brain or organ damage". But, after this experience, I KNEW how I would be, where I would be, the freedom I would feel if I died and was not in my body anymore.

I became extremely suicidal, yearning "for God" again, fully knowing who He was and the love, peace and freedom of being in that state of awareness. Needless to say, I wanted to be back in that condition again and I did not remember at all how I was able to have my soul leave my physical body as it did before. I was devastated that I forgot how. . After this experience, I completely lost any and all fear of death. In fact, I yearned for it more than I can express. I knew my body was not who I really was and I wanted myself back again – my true self. I knew what this was after this experience.

Connie

Message from Heaven #154
This out of the body experience Connie had can happen every night during your sleep. When your awareness starts expanding, this will happen

automatically more often. In time, this will begin to happen when you are awake, not only when sleeping.

Your awareness, which is now confined within your body, will expand beyond those physical limitations. When this happens, it is at first enlightening. Limitation is not present anymore. It is a feeling of utter and invigorating freedom.

This awareness that you speak of is who you really are. It is your eternal self. It is the awareness of your soul. There is no fear within your soul's awareness and the freedom from fear is what you felt. You are intended to experience this loving state of awareness while you are living in your physical body. You are here to experience life in a physical world while simultaneously maintaining full awareness of your true self. This means all fear within your awareness is fully healed. As you heal more fear, your consciousness expands and you become more of who you really are – fearless and God realized, free of pain and suffering. The love, bliss and peace of who you are is fully there in your awareness now.

Imagine living your lives in this natural state of awareness. There is no such thing as fear or limitation. You know God is everywhere. You can experience anything you want to, literally. That's why you are here on earth; to experience what you want to for the fun and joy of it. The only thing that keeps your full awareness from being experienced is your fear. Until you heal it all, you will be limited. Face your fears as I did and become free hearted and fully God realized. This is your natural state of experience.

Jesus

Lost and Confused

Message from Heaven #155

I WOULD NOW like to talk about something new; about your parents; your birth mother and father. I'd like to explain about the verse you have heard to honor your mother and father. I want to explain why. Some of you have had parents who did not honor you. Some even abused you, abandoned you and broke your heart. And, you are still living with that unhealed pain to this very day.

I want you to know that your soul asked their soul to be your mother or father, and that they agreed to do so out of pure love for you. Some of you have chosen to believe in pain and suffering. Therefore, you will create it one way or another. When you are ready to say good bye to such pain, you will be done with it. You will simply not attract it anymore. The Universe will support this healing transformation in your heart automatically, as it always does. It is the law of the Universe. This is how our Father created you – as creators yourself. What you believe in, you will experience. And if you believe you deserve pain, even if only unconsciously, the universe will coordinate events for you to match that belief. This is the law of creation.

There is also the law of cause and effect; what some of you call karma. It is true that what you give out in the form of your thoughts, feelings or actions, you will also receive back. These parents will receive what they need to learn compassion. Have compassion for all, including those who hurt you the most. They are the ones that loved you enough to give you the experience you needed to learn how to grow to a higher level of loving.
Jesus

Message from Heaven #156

I will now talk to these parents who know who they are; the parents who harmed their children by neglecting their role as a loving, caring parent. Your hidden shame will do nothing of value. Your hiding the truth, living in self-deceit, will do nothing of value. Continuing to live with this level of guilt brings you more self-sacrifice than you know.

I want to help you free yourself of this. However you choose to hide this truth will bring a painful disillusionment to you. The longer you carry it, the deeper experience this will be. Remember that carrying an unhealed fear continues to strengthen it.

To bring light to this, help children with the same hurts you caused to your own. Make them your priority for the rest of your life. Help these children heal. Help them be prosperous. Help them be loved. Also, give me your lack of forgiveness toward others and ask me to help you forgive yourself.
Jesus

Message from Heaven #157

Are you going to become more numb now, or are you going to listen to my suggestion? Ignorance is self-chosen and keeps you in the cycle of fear. For those who did not neglect your children this way, know that there is someone to whom you gave unkindness. Do not listen to your ego telling you this does not include you, so that you can stay stuck in spiritual stagnation. This includes every one of you. Feel guilt not. Bring light to it instead. Forgive yourself for not knowing how to love more like me yet. Know that you have my forgiveness already. Know that you need your own forgiveness to become free like me.

Since it is your own self-judgment that created this, know that you cannot resolve it without our Father. Self-forgiveness is needed to become free. Ask me to help you forgive any wrong you have done. Ask me to help you heal it. Do not ask and then forget about it. You need to bring action into it; action that is loving. The way to forgive yourself of anything, is to intentionally give love to others. Helping others heal and become free of disharmony, pain, emptiness, lack and limitation is to free yourself of all of those fearful qualities.

With genuine intention behind your words to me, I will set you free. Come up to me and my way of living. This means actively loving. Freedom is on the other side of all misdoings when you are giving love intentionally.
Jesus

Message from Heaven #158

When are you going to decide to wake up? When you are forced to? You can bring grace into your past and present misgivings with self-honesty. When you no longer avoid facing the truth of the unloving energy you have extended to others, including yourself, I will bring grace into your life. This means only with your acceptance. This grace brings immediate peace and allows love to expand more within you. This is our Father's love, so remember to thank Him for it.

This message is about self-awareness – having enough intentional self-awareness to be honest with yourself. When you avoid facing your truth because you fear it so much, you are strengthening and empowering this fear within you. In time, this brings you to your knees. But know it is unnecessary to undergo this painful experience. Choose to face your fears instead, including deep ones that you intentionally ignore and pretend are not there. Know this is what I did to become as I am; fully united with our Father and all. The kingdom of God is within you already. It will be realized by you when you honor your fears.
Jesus

New Patterns

Message from Heaven #159

QUESTION FROM CONNIE: Jesus, some of the readers of "*Messages from Heaven*" Facebook page have some questions for you about forming the communities you recommend. For those who may be interested in this, would you please explain in more detail what these communities would be like? Some have asked if they would be required to separate themselves from the rest of world; if it would be clannish or like a "cult". Could you please comment?

Jesus: I would like my communities to have complete and total freedom from all forms of restrictions and limitations. This includes loving and welcoming all within and to all those who are outside of the community. However, the community should not house more than 300 people as I have previously discussed.

I would like it to be what you might call a development, neighborhood, subdivision or small village. There would be homes on the property for the residents who live there, a healing facility that focuses on the emotional healing of one's suppressed pain and fear, a "town center" or town hub, where there are some stores, offices, rooms for teaching children and adults, and other small businesses within the community, such as a store to trade goods, a dentist, doctor and veterinarian office, etc. It is up to the residents of the community to choose exactly what stores or rooms they would like to have available in the community, as well as the preferred design of the community. But, I will give you some specific suggestions you may want to consider:

1) A store with extra and left over food that has been grown, prepared and stored from each household that would like to share or trade

with their neighbors. For example, one can trade their eggs for a neighbor's apples; their grown walnuts for your vegetables.
2) A healing facility for emotional healing.
3) A doctor, dentist and veterinarian office for the use of the residents of the community.
4) You, Connie, have already 'envisioned' a quaint, charming store that makes non-toxic, luxury hand-made soap, laundry and dish detergent, shampoos and conditioner, lotions and creams, beautiful candles, raw dairy products and a fitness center...etc.
5) A store with supplies of equipment and tools to build; a place to make and repair things.

Jesus

Message from Heaven #160

When you are feeling lonely, what do you think you need? What does your mind tell you? Pay attention to this. Your mind will think of something in the physical world: a person, a situation or a thing. Notice this. I have already explained how anything from the physical plane cannot satisfy or fulfill your heart's yearning for fullness. But, notice how you continue the same pattern of thinking; thinking you need something more 'out there' to bring you more peace, security, happiness, freedom, wholeness and love.

Know that when you ask God for these "things", you are telling Him (reinforcing) it is not Him who you want and need, but the things He can bring you. This is staying stuck in the unfulfilling pattern of ego's thinking. Ego always wants something more from the physical plane. Ego comes from your mind, God comes through your heart. Your heart always wants God - the qualities that come from love – compassion, kindness, happiness, joy, peace, wholeness.

Yet, your mind continues to believe you need something from the physical plane for your fulfillment. This unconscious, habitual pattern of thinking has been going on for a long period of time. You are still stuck in this same pattern of thinking and living and have not as yet achieved fulfillment. Recognizing this will change your life. The simple awareness of this will be life-changing. I now ask you to bring your awareness to this without the usual negative self-judgment.

After reading this message, spend a few minutes and ask yourself what you think you need to *not* feel that underlying loneliness deep inside. It is always there - that feeling of something missing. I'd like you to become more aware of it. Give it a few moments of your attention please. What does your mind tell you must happen to fill that emptiness? It is important to write down your answers. List them individually.

Now, say something like this to me: "Jesus, I am lost. I do not know how to bring my heart fullness. I am confused about how to create true happiness and fulfillment. I live in a physical world and have physical needs. But, I am confused about how to attain fullness of life. Since I do not yet experience fullness of life, I must not know how to create it. But, I want to know. I want to know how to feel complete, wholly loved, fully lovable and instilled with your level of inner peace, joy and love in my heart – what you call, "fullness of life". I am asking you to help me with this since I do not know how."
Jesus

Message from Heaven #161

Do you understand better now, how the ego will always keep you in a state of wanting fulfillment but never achieving it? And, that it is never ending? Ego will never feel good enough. Ego believes nothing is good enough. And, that also will always be this way. Remember that ego believes it is separate from fullness. However, intellectually understanding this will not stop its' continuing control of your thinking.

The only way to turn around the ego's fear is to honor it. Acknowledge how it feels. Give it your full attention, especially when it gets stronger. Talk to your ego as if it were an actual being, because it is. Accept it and literally tell it you understand how it feels. Tell your ego it has a valid reason for feeling this way. This gives it your acceptance. Now, feel its fear. Feel it as fully as you can. Then talk to me a few minutes about it. Tell me what you acknowledge. Tell me how it, your ego, makes you feel. Then surrender that painful feeling to me and simply ask me to free you of it. Put it in my hands now for me to take care of.

This simple action of acceptance and surrender is all you need to change the pattern of the ego's habitual fearful thinking that, right now, is automatic. Doing this daily, or more frequently as needed, creates a new thought pattern that will not allow the ego to keep **you** stuck in feeling **its** fear. Worry not. Doing this will develop your trust in Me. Worry dissolves as you develop your trust in Me.
Jesus

Message from Heaven #162

Any concern you ever have should be given to me to take care of for you. This develops a new way of living – intentionally surrendering your every concern or need to me. This will bring the letting go of ego automatically – without even trying. Remember that trying to resist ego will never work. Resisting ego always makes it stronger. Through intentional surrender, you simply become less dependent on the ego to govern your life. Here, when I say ego, I mean your mind. I want you to transition from your mind controlling your thinking to your heart directing your life. This is the way to begin.

Tell me what you need help with throughout your day. Give me your needs, your concerns, your fears. Give them all to me and ask me to take care of them for you. Surrendering your life to our Father begins like this. It is so simple that many may ignore this message, thinking this could make little or no difference. Please remember that if you stay thinking the same way, you will continue to stagnate as you have been. The conditions on earth have not improved, they have grown worse. This is because the collective consciousness of earth's inhabitants is devolving. You are all connected and you all affect each other's growth more than you know.

Surrendering the desire to control everything and giving it to me instead, brings in more peace. So, when you notice you are feeling fearful, worried or frustrated, give me your concerns right then in that very moment. Ask me to resolve it as I would like it to be. Trust in me to do a better job than you. Many want to know how to bring more peace and grace into their lives and dissolve the ego's resistance and fear. This is an ideal way to begin.
Jesus

Message from Heaven #163

When you are feeling sad, I'd like you to give your sadness some undistracted attention. Too often, when the sadness in your heart comes to the surface to be acknowledged, felt and loved, you avoid it. You do not want to feel it. Know that ignoring it this way strengthens the sadness. This wreaks havoc in your life in every way imaginable and diminishes your inner joy in every moment.

I want to help you know how to get your true state of experience back. Your unhealed fear must be dealt with to accomplish this. I know many of you do not want to hear about this. You want to continue to ignore it. Ignoring it seems to make you feel better than facing it. But, know that is far from the truth. It is unnatural to age in the way most of you do. It is unnatural to feel less than in love with life every moment. It is unnatural to have fear. It is unnatural to feel less than loving. It is unnatural to be sad. These feelings are not from God – from love. They are symptoms that occur from the not knowing of who you are. When you realize that you are love itself and are not separate from anything or anyone, including our Father, there is no such thing as sadness. Yet, you are so used to having these feelings, you have come to believe they are 'natural'.

I know you cannot understand an existence without pain and suffering yet. Know I am sharing these messages to help you grow beyond this. When you are ready for God-realization, you will be ready to listen to new knowledge that can help you grow. Until then, I can offer you little assistance. If you choose to stay stuck in your present way of thinking and living, I sit back and wait for your readiness to grow more.

Reaching your potential requires acknowledging what you have adopted that is not real. Anything that does not come from love is not real. This includes sadness. If you were to honor your feelings of sadness as they arise, rather than pretending they are not there, they would begin to dissolve, simply by facing them. It can be a very simple process to heal away all the suppressed pain and fear you have accumulated from your many lifetimes. You simply give your sorrowful feelings a little time each day to be acknowledged, honored and felt. This is giving it awareness, acceptance and love. It is our Father's love which will then heal and dissolve those feelings. But, you have to be willing to give acceptance.

Give the sorrow within you just a little undistracted time each day. Allow yourself to feel it. Honor it. Face it and you will free yourself of it and all of the limitations you have unknowingly taken on because of it. Know that you will not fully understand the value of this until you start to experience the benefits. Our Father wants to blossom within you. This means His love, peace and joy. He wants to experience Himself through you fully. When you face what is not real, truth will prevail.
Jesus

Message from Heaven #164

I would now like to discuss how to cultivate inner joy. The level of inner joy you experience has been dramatically reduced. Most of you believe that when something you consider 'good' happens, that it is **that particular experience** which caused more inner joy. Notice how this increased inner joy is very temporary. Your ego brings you back to feeling something isn't good enough again and then it tries to figure out something else you need to make you feel more inner joy again.

This inconsistent inner joy is very superficial. It is also a very limited level of inner joy. Since this is all you know, you think it is normal. Yes, it is natural to enjoy your physical experiences and they are intended to be enjoyed. But, I want to help you know there is a level of inner joy that has nothing to do with the outer world. It is an experience that most of you do not know.

This is the inner joy that comes from our Father expressing through you – experiencing Himself through you. It has nothing to do with what occurs in the material world. Experiencing God's inner joy is not dependent on what is happening outside of you. To explain it simply, it is dependent only on how much of your Love Energy [God's energy] is flowing through you; within your heart and consciousness.

If you were to put your attention on the Love Energy that is flowing through you, rather than on what experience you can get from the physical world to give you more inner joy, your life would change dramatically. You would change from a life of trials and tribulations, fear and limitations of every kind, to a fulfilling life where you are the master of every moment. You are intended to be masters of your lives rather than your lives being masters over you and your feelings. You can allow God to create every step of the way before you. He wants to give you what He has to offer. But unknowingly, you do not understand what He has to give. You would rather settle for what you think is better than God Himself – something transitory from the physical world.

I know you do not understand how you are doing this – rejecting God. You do not think you are. Do not judge yourself for this. Do not judge yourself for what you do not yet understand. You are learning how to be with God in your awareness. Reading these messages are helping you with this.

Become more interested in how you can experience the inner joy that comes only from bringing more Love Energy through you; more of my awareness of our Father's love through you. Do not believe what you have been taught for many centuries; that you have to sacrifice the abundance of anything for God. This is a mistaken belief. It is the extreme opposite.

To bring more awareness of God into your life you need to spend a little time thinking this: *"How can I experience more of our Father's love through my heart and consciousness"*? It is necessary for you to want this in order to receive it. It is necessary to want His level of inner joy in order to experience it. Otherwise, you will stay as you are, extremely limited and controlled by your outer world, living perpetually as victims of circumstance. Rise above that. Be all of who you are intended to be. Ask yourself how you can experience more of God's love. Giving it is what will bring you more of His level of love; more of God's inner joy into each and every one of your experiences.

Try a new way of living for a little while. See what happens in your lives and your world. Instead of living for the experience your ego thinks you need, live for the purpose of experiencing more Love Energy. This is putting your love first, which will then create your loving experiences. This is putting God first. This is allowing God to create your life.
Jesus

Message from Heaven #165
Believe in your worthiness to receive God's grace. How do you do this when there is an underlying core belief within you that feels not good

enough for God? You simply remind yourself that you are, every day throughout the day.

Tell yourself and God that you know He wants you to be in love with your life; that you are intended to experience love and joy to fullness – which in unlimited. The love and joy within you can continue to grow. There is no end to the love and joy of our Father. Watch what you think of that is not in alignment with feeling love and joy - negative, fearful thinking. Pay attention to these thoughts. They create your reality.

Every time you have a fearful thought, a negative thought, one of worry, judgment or disapproval of another; one of jealously or of guilt or any kind of disharmony, say this to me:

"God, I know you want me to fall in love with my life. My ego just had another fear-based thought, but I know not to believe it. I know I am deserving of all the love and joy our Father wants to give me. Take this thought from me and give me the ability to think more like you. I want to. Thank you."

It can be this simple to start changing your thoughts. This brings your awareness to those random thoughts that usually go on without you even noticing them. It is this simple to begin a new pattern of thinking. If you do not change the quality of your thoughts, you will not be able to love more. It is as simple as that. It is love that brings you closer to your higher self's awareness. Bring more love and self-worthiness into your beliefs by noticing your less than loving thoughts as they arise. Then give them to me to transform.
Jesus

Message from Heaven #166
You begin to create a new pattern of correcting your fear-based thoughts by noticing them as they arise and then surrendering them to me to transform into a loving thought. From time to time, start thanking me for changing your thinking. Thank me for improving the quality of your thoughts. Acknowledge that I am doing this for you now because you are now noticing them and giving them to me to heal. Remember that I am healing the quality of your thoughts, not you. Remember that you are not able to heal them yourself right now, because you are the one that is

thinking them. It is I who heals them for you. Say something like this to me throughout the day:

"*Thank you Jesus for healing my thoughts. I know I do not know how to heal them right now. Thank you*".

Saying this to me several times a day is acknowledging that I am. Your consciousness needs to know this change is taking place to make it a reality. Remember that your consciousness creates your reality. If you want to change your reality, you have to change your consciousness.

Jesus

Message from Heaven #167

When you become capable of feeling more inner joy, a miracle occurs. You are in the flow of the divine. You experience more of the divine. What needs to be healed becomes healed. Your life is restored as your fears leave you. The fears are replaced with love. An ease and grace enter your direct experience now. The synchronicities are at first mystifying. You know this is not coming from you alone, but from something within you. It is divine.

You detach yourself from damaging thoughts, feelings and behaviors spontaneously. Loving energy now replaces them. You become familiar with my way of thinking, feeling and behaving. Less fear, less judgment and dysfunction. There is more and more love. Miracles now occur rapidly in your life - all which work to further the experience of more love, more abundance, and more joy.

Jesus

Message from Heaven #168

When you are at a time where this flow of inner joy becomes stronger, changes in your life are around the corner. Sometimes relationships, situations and other circumstances start to fall apart. Because you may judge the dissolving away of these situations as "bad" and then fear this process, chaos comes into your life.

The increased inner joy you had developed (which is creating these changes) goes away again as fear becomes predominant. Your conditioned response is to resist these changes and try to prevent them. Ego has now taken over your life once again. This creates pain and suffering and problems; chaos and disharmony.

You are losing what is no longer beneficial for you because you are ready to attract a higher experience. This means more love, abundance and inner joy. You have out grown what you previously attracted. This is a time to celebrate and to give thanks to our Father for helping you grow into being more of who you are.

But, your ego perceives this differently. Developing more God energy within you, which is the energy and presence of love, peace and inner joy, dissolves the ego's fear. Ego's survival instincts then become stronger.

If you believe in what the ego perceives – that these changes are bad, that you are losing something good and that you have to stop and fix these unwanted changes - you will lose the progress you have made. You will go backwards once again, losing the increased God energy you had developed.

This back and forth battle between love and fear is what some call having an angel and a devil on your shoulder. I would like to help you understand how to perceive these times of spiritual growth with more truth. Watch yourself during these times of transition, from a present experience to a new experience, as if you are a third party and not at all involved in the experience. Simply witness yourself during this time. Have intentional awareness of your human-self experiencing these life changes.

This intentional conscious awareness of your human-self automatically transitions your perception from ego toward love; from fear to trust; from judgment to surrender; from resistance to acceptance. I call this detachment from ego, freedom. It is freedom from the limitation of ego.
When you start to become more fearful, more judgmental, more at a place of resisting 'what is', intentionally watch yourself from the perspective of a witness. Become aware of your higher-self's awareness by watching your human self's experience.
Jesus

Heaven in Your Heart

Message from Heaven #169

I WOULD LIKE TO discuss Heaven. Heaven has been misunderstood for thousands of years. I have previously discussed this but I would like to discuss it further now. Many think that heaven is a place you go to after you die if you were 'good' enough in your lifetime. Some believe only the people of their own religious belief get there. Some think it's a place where God exists. Others believe there is no such thing.

I want you to understand that heaven is a state of awareness that contains no fear. Heaven is having the full awareness of God; the presence of God's love. It is a mind-set, a perception that is all loving. When one reaches this state of awareness, they have developed Christ consciousness – a fully loving consciousness. There is no more fear in their perception. Their heart is fully healed of all their painful experiences. Their heart is fully open and loving. The presence of fear is gone.

Fear manifests in many different ways and consists of the belief that you are separate from God. You are born with the limited awareness that you are separate from God, from others and all else. Your soul wanted to experience and express the love that it is. Instead of knowing you are all one as you are, you wanted the experience of learning this. If you already know you are one, you cannot experience the joy of learning that you are not separate. It is the singular joy of falling in love with God.

When your soul enters a fetus, you start experiencing yourself as a separate individual. Learning that you are all the same love energy experiencing individual lives is 'physical life'. You are not only love energy being itself, you can experience your love energy. The joy of expressing who you are – love energy, is the greatest gift imaginable. But, when you begin fearing the separateness of your existence, ego is born.

Ego is a perception of resistance to whatever is. It is pure resistance. You fear yourself upon this moment. The resistance indicates fear is present. It shows you are not accepting of whatever is happening and that you fear having to deal with it. You fear you are not able or good enough. You could face this fear instantly by not resisting it; that is, not trying to control, manipulate or avoid it.

But, if you reject this separating experience and follow your fear instead, fear is in your perception. The more you follow your fear and listen to it, allow it to control your perception, the stronger and more influential it becomes. It is your formless fear that creates all pain and suffering in your existence – for each and every one of you. You do not know there is another perception available – my perception – Christ consciousness. There is no such thing as pain and suffering when you have developed my perception – my awareness.

You could continue living many more lives unknowingly stuck in your fearful perception. You would then continue living more lives experiencing pain and suffering in various ways. There is another choice available – my way of living. You will eventually accept it, but the when of it is up to you. I am communicating to you through Connie and others at this time, to help you learn how to let go of your fear and allow our Father's love to flow through you fully.

You must first want this to receive this different awareness; this different perception. This includes a different way of thinking. Altering the way you think is a necessity. When you allow your mind to start thinking more like my way of thinking, you allow your heart's love to expand within you. This is our Father. Acceptance from you is all that is needed; the acceptance to change your thinking. No one achieves the experience of Heaven until their thoughts are fully loving. How do you achieve only fully loving thoughts? By healing all of the suppressed pain and fear you have experienced. You have to address your unhealed pain and fear from your past. The *HOPE Technique* is the method I created for accomplishing this.

If you gave yourself a little time each day to do the *HOPE Technique*, you would quickly be at a different level of awareness. Love would continue to

heal your heart again and again until your fears are no more. It can be this simple.
Jesus

Message from Heaven #170
When you effectively heal your past hurts – the remaining unhealed pain in your heart - freedom is near. At first, you feel worse. You are feeling all the pain and fear you have been avoiding your whole life. If you can allow yourself to go through this process anyway, you would soon reach a place of acceptance with it. This is the moment I am waiting for with each of you. This is the moment you allow God to heal you. This is the moment you step out from the state of ignorance. This is when your true self starts to shine from inside.

I have given you the *HOPE Technique* to help you through this process; to make the process of deep emotional healing simple and effective. But, it still requires courage to do it. Remaining in a state of ignorance from what needs to be healed appears easier on the surface. But remember that ignoring and avoiding something does not make it go away. It actually strengthens its' hold on you.

Until you are willing to face and feel your unhealed pain and fear, you will continue living in ignorance. This means living in ignorance of the direct experience of God. And this means living with trials and tribulations; pain and suffering; an emptiness that will never go away until you realize God. Until you face what is preventing you from experiencing God – your pain and fear – you will live in a painful, fearful and separating existence.

I have given you a way to find freedom from ignorance of God's love. The *HOPE Technique* heals what is covering it up - your pain and fear. The *Heart Technique* stills the mind's thoughts and connects you directly to your soul's awareness. All it requires is a little time each day for doing it.
Jesus

Message from Heaven #171

A most beautiful experience awaits you when you are healing your pain and fear. It is God's loving energy expanding within you. You are allowing God to heal your fear when you are doing the *HOPE Technique*. As more fear dissolves away, more love expands. You are in the process of becoming free hearted – like a child again. Nothing and no one in the physical world can give you this experience. Nothing from the physical world can compare to this. The awakening of God's love within you is the most beautiful feeling imaginable.

When I was on earth as Jesus Christ, I tried to teach you that your fear is not real; that it is an illusion you believe in. And that facing it rather than trying to avoid it is what will set you free from it. Try a new way of living for a little while. See what happens in your life. If you want to go back to ignoring what you are avoiding, you can. Trust in me if only for a little while. See what becomes of it. Resist evil not. This means not to resist your fears and to face them instead.

Using the *HOPE Technique* helps make this healing process simple and effective.

Jesus

Angel's Speak

Message from Heaven #172

I AM AN **angel of love. I would like to impart my knowledge of how to fall in love with your life.** It is easy for me to love my life because I am never not loving. I accept whatever God creates for me always. I never judge what God creates for me. I accept everything I experience with deep gratitude, whatever it may be. I too, have preferences about my experiences. I would rather be assigned to help an already loving, kind person to become more loving. It is a more enjoyable experience for me to help someone who has more love developed at the beginning.

But, sometimes I am given a very unloving person to help. They are filled with anger, hate and resentment or deep self-pity, worry and fear. My purpose, as the angel I am, is to influence my human friend toward wanting to be more loving. This could mean to be more loving of another person, themselves or a situation in their life. I stay near them and the energy which emanates from my being affects them positively. It enhances the energy they emanate from their being.

Every being's inner energy extends outward and influences the experience in which they are presently involved. Humans often do not understand how easy it is to accept what they are experiencing in each moment. They have an automatic tendency to judge whatever they are experiencing as not being good enough. Then, they put their thoughts and energy toward talking and complaining about it, thinking how they can change it, improve it or make it go away so they can control their experience to be something different than what it is. Most humans do this continuously. They do not even realize they are doing this. It has become such a habit, they do not understand that they are resisting God's desires and God's will all the time.

They think they can improve themselves, their circumstances or someone in their life. This then becomes their mission – trying to decide who or what is not good enough and how to correct and improve it all. They do not understand that if they chose to accept their present experience exactly as it is, they would not feel unhappy, dissatisfied or resentful about it. It is their judgment that brings them unhappiness, not the person or situation they are dealing with.

Most humans have developed this mind set and they are rarely happy or satisfied with their lives as a result. It is interesting for me to witness how they perceive what God gives them as unsatisfactory. They habitually try to change "whatever is". They unknowingly create their own misery. I simply stay near them so my loving energy will influence them positively. My presence does help them as many would be even unhappier without it. Because you are part of me and I love you, I do want you to be happier. This is a natural desire I have for all beings; for all to be in love with their lives. As your happiness grows, so does mine. I am still completely happy even when you are not. But, my soul radiates more love when you spread your love more. We are connected in this way naturally.

I usually do not have the opportunity to explain this to humans. I am pleased God has given me this opportunity so you may be more understanding of this self-defeating thinking process. I hope to help you realize how you can change your perception of any experience.

I would like to give you some different examples of how you unknowingly reduce your love and happiness feelings from your experiences. I desire this opportunity to speak of how I perceive. Perceiving like me and most angels will create the very experiences your soul wants you to have. Until you learn how to perceive more like me, you cannot create these higher, more loving experiences for yourself.

As I share some experiences I have witnessed, I am offering you a loving way of perceiving them. Know that if you allow yourself to perceive more like me, you will not need the limited, or painful experiences you have so long endured. They will fizzle out because your energy of dissatisfaction will not continue to fuel your perception, which further escalate those limited, unsatisfying experiences.

Witnessed Experience from an "Angel of love" (example #1): I was once with a human who was very judgmental toward people who were less educated than he. He had been raised with the belief that only people who were more highly educated (as he) were worthy of honor, respect, and his time and consideration - which means his love. He experienced so much dissatisfaction throughout his life. Except for those people who had a similar level of education he had, he constantly judged everyone he came into contact with as not good enough for his love and kindness.

He grew more and more discontent with his life because he was discontented with most people. He couldn't connect the dots. He had no idea how he was creating more and more discontented experiences for himself. He negatively judged most people as not being good enough, always looking down on them, so he disliked most people. He grew to dislike his own life more and more as a result. All of a sudden, he started losing the people he did like – the more educated people. His business partner betrayed him. He lost him as a business partner and friend and he lost much money as well. This led to losing more of his money and then his business.

This process took a few years to result in a state of mental anguish and physical breakdown. He created the loss of his wife and children for he did not appreciate all the love and happy experiences that were available to him from his family. He did not feel loving to them and often times he was rude to them. They felt more and more hurt and then resentful. More and more he judged his wife as not good enough. He criticized her more and more. The wife came to despise her husband and chose to love another man instead. Her husband grew to hate her and she hated him so much at this point, she did something intentionally hurtful to him. She embarrassed him in public around many of his educated friends. She knew this would upset him more than anything. She wanted him to suffer the same humiliation, hurt and rejection that she felt. He lost every single one of these friends. They now judged him as not good enough for their respect, time or love.

This man was now without his business which he had so loved working at. He was without the friendship of his business partner and his wife and children. His family did not even want to be around him anymore. He lost his house that he had enjoyed living in very much and all of his activities were unavailable to him now because all of his friends, business relationships and family were lost to him.

He was in a hotel room by himself and was so engulfed in hatred for himself and his life that he thought about killing himself. Then he did. These years of more and more intense misery and loss resulted from his judgmental beliefs that less educated people were not good enough and therefore, not worthy of his time, respect or love.

If he were to have changed his perception about less educated people many years ago, he could have experienced a treasure trove of so many loving and joyful times. He could have chosen to perceive all these people and all his situations with love and appreciation instead. But, he did not. His own perception continued to create more and more judgment of everything in his life as unacceptable until he could not live with himself and all that he created. Many people have this same judgment toward others but for reasons other than education. Some people feel others are not good enough because they:

a) wear different clothes
b) have different beliefs
c) have a different type of personality
d) are not as athletic as they are
f) are not good looking enough
g) do not have as much money
h) have a different type of profession
i) don't have a house or car they feel is equivalent to theirs
j) have a health issue they don't have
k) are too old
l) are too young
m) were born in a country they feel is not good enough
n) do not have more friends

o) have different hobbies or interests they disapprove of
p) don't wear nice jewelry
q) have a different skin color
r) have a different religion
s) have a different social status

I have seen so many reasons people choose to perceive others as not good enough. The result is always the same. They create a "not good enough" life for themselves.
"Angel of love"

Message from Heaven #173

Witnessed Experience from an "Angel of love" (example #2): I once helped a human who had a lot of judgment toward himself. He felt he was not good enough for many reasons. He felt inferior all the time. His father was particularly judgmental toward him, although his father did not express that openly to others. His father felt very inferior. He often judged others as not being good enough for many different reasons, talked negatively about others behind their backs and enjoyed making people feel inferior, including his son. This was unconscious on his part. He could not connect the dots.

His father's pattern of thinking, talking and behavior was habitually focused on how other people were not good enough. As a result, he strongly influenced his son's beliefs about himself as being not good enough. This helped his father cover up his feelings of himself not being good enough. He chose to continue to ignore his fears of not being good enough, so the fears continued to escalate. The son's father never acknowledged or expressed approval for any of his son's accomplishments. Whatever the son did or accomplished, his father would tell him how he could have done it better. The son grew up believing he was never good enough and he continuously strived to accomplish more.

When the son became a young adult, he became my human friend to be helped. He was headed toward creating much suffering. He was soon going to attract a wife who also felt very inferior about herself and lived her life seeking other people's approval and love. This gave her a false sense of feeling loved, cared for and approved of. She rarely received this from her mother throughout her childhood. She also ignored facing her fears of not being good enough. There would have been nothing she could do that would have been good enough in her husband's opinion. This woman would have become an alcoholic if she had married him. This would have helped her cope with the painful feelings of not being good enough in the eyes of her husband. She would have created much self-loathing, sickness and unhappiness.

This marriage would have resulted in a lot of misery for each other, as well as bringing a baby into the world born with a physical and mental defect from the mother drinking alcohol. It would have been a very unhappy life for the husband, wife and their child, experiencing much hardship in various ways. They would also have perpetuated much suffering for many other people who they came into contact with throughout their lives.

However, the influence of my loving energy being near this man, my human friend, helped him very much. He was able to accept a different perception about himself. He was able to accept loving himself more and more from the influence of my loving energy. His life went in a completely different direction as a result.

His increased loving energy changed the way he thought about himself and other people. He became one of the most loving and non-judgmental humans I have been assigned to help. I blossomed with much love and joy from the love energy he was willing to accept for himself and extend to others. I had much fun helping him love himself more and more. He was one of my favorite experiences. He helped so many people become happier and love themselves more. He helped people heal their self-loathing. He had such a happy life with his wife and four children. He loved and appreciated them so much. He demonstrated how to love them too. He honored their feelings and encouraged them to honor their feelings also.

This man had a choice to make when I was assigned to him. He could have chosen to continue feeling not good enough about himself and others. Instead, he began to perceive himself with love and acceptance and appreciate the qualities he had that he liked. He chose to perceive his life with more

and more appreciation. I am so pleased he chose to love himself, his life and other people more, instead of continuing to perceive as his father did – as everyone and everything was not good enough.
"Angel of love"

Message from Heaven #174

I am an angel of power. I specialize in giving people the power that comes from loving themselves more. It is a quality that comes from love. I am given a human to help positively influence their feelings of being unable to love themselves more. Typically, the humans I am given to help are doormats. They have extreme feelings of unworthiness. So much so, they allow people to treat them very poorly. They are stuck in a situation where someone in their life treats them with disrespect and mistreatment in one way or another.

The humans I receive to help need my influence greatly. You could say, I am given more severe cases. I have a powerful influence on them. I help them start to think differently about themselves. I help them want to have a better, happier life. I help them think outside a box of extreme self-limitation.

Most of the people I am given to influence have had a long history of accepting mistreatment from others. At first, they do not even think about being capable of creating a better, happier life. They feel that unworthy; so unworthy, they do not even think about the possibility of a higher experience. They always think they cannot have a happier life for one reason or another. They are stuck in that deeply imbedded belief.

Since love energy has a power to it, it promotes a feeling from within that naturally wants happiness. I intentionally emanate this quality that comes from love – the desire to be happy. This is automatic and natural for most people. But, the people I am given to help, have suppressed this desire. They have fully accepted that they are not worthy of being happy at all whatsoever. I shine my love on them so much and I love every minute of my work. It is so exciting for me to see my love energy start to influence their thinking. I help them think about having a happier life.

In time, they start questioning their beliefs that they are not worthy of being happy. Then they start thinking of having a different experience – a happier experience. This is when I start doing flips and cart wheels. I am so happy to see them become open to receiving more abundance in their mind set now. This is when I can really help them get out of an unhappy situation. They are now ready to accept more happiness. I love my life. I love helping people become happy. It is such a joyful experience for me. I love being able to share my love with others. I am very good at it.

When the human I am helping gets to this point of readiness to receive more happiness, my work with them is done. A different angel then comes to give them a different influence – strength and courage. I am then assigned another human to help in the same way. I have never failed at my work – not even with one human. I am very happy about that. I love being Jesus' helper. He has many angel helpers. He gives us those humans who need our qualities. We serve Him and you with great appreciation. It is a blessing to help people become happier. It keeps us shining with love and joy.

I'd like to tell you that if you are presently this doormat type of person, who allows others to mistreat you in some way, the most helpful thing you can do other than asking Jesus to help you, is to start thinking differently about your past. All the people I am given to help, fully believe that they cannot have only loving, kind people in their life because of their past experiences. They think that because they grew up with an unloving, unkind mother, father or other family member who mistreated them; that this is who they are – someone who is meant to be mistreated. They simply accept that belief. So, they continue attracting other people in their life who also mistreat them.

If you are one of these people, know that **your present experience creates your future experiences.** So, if you presently think you can have only people in your life that treat you well and with love and respect, you will automatically change your future experiences to creating exactly that. Your damaging relationships will begin to dissolve away or transform into healthy and loving relationships.

Think and believe that in your life you **can have** only those people who honor you, love you and treat you well. I can say that if you presently believe this is possible for you, regardless of what past experiences you have had,

your life will begin to transform into attracting and creating relationships with people that treat you well. Just believing this is possible for you in your present experience is all that is needed to bypass needing an angel like me to help you achieve this perception. You will be one big step ahead toward creating beautiful, loving and happy relationships.
"Angel of the power of love"

Message from Heaven #175
I am an angel that specializes in helping people who are angry. I am only given people who are very angry towards other people. I support coordinating events for my human friend that will help them realize their anger is a result of their own behavior and not the behavior of others. I intentionally bring them an experience that will snap them out of this judgmental perception toward others.

I have the ability to love without guilt. The people who I am assigned to help, have extreme guilt. This is why they have so much anger toward other people. They cannot bear to face their own guilt, so they choose to judge and condemn other people harshly instead. This helps them feel self-righteous. Self-righteousness is a delusional mind-made perception that helps one escape their truth; the truth of their own guilt, which they prefer to ignore.

They do not want to face their incorrect way of thinking. If they did, they would realize they have been creating their own misery, and usually for a long time. They simply do not want to accept this responsibility. If they did, they would feel the pain of knowing they behaved un-lovingly to their brothers and sisters. This would be the painful feelings of guilt. Facing this guilt would lead to knowing they have hurt their Creator. They have avoided facing this at any cost by the time I am assigned to help them.

Most humans on earth do not understand that being unkind, unloving or judgmental toward someone is rejecting God. It is rejecting their own Creator. Everyone is God, though in a different physical form. Being an angel, I am God in a non-physical form. My form consists of a less dense energy than your highly dense human form. We are all God experiencing the love energy we are, through a form. God feels what every being feels. So, when you judge, hurt or reject others, God feels that too.

When I am given a human to help, I determine what type of people they judge and dislike the most, for this is the very quality they have much of. Feeling anger toward another is always due to something the person has within their consciousness that is not in alignment with love. I bring them the awareness of exactly what that is. You could say, I bring them a big wake up call. It is a very disillusioning experience for them to realize they are the problem, not the other person(s).

They resist their truth and it brings them much unnecessary pain and suffering. I came to talk to you to help humans understand that it is OK to acknowledge that you have been thinking and behaving in an unloving manner. When you recognize this truth, it is a time to celebrate and rejoice, not condemn yourself. You are closer to realizing what prevents you from being all-loving. That is a beautiful time to appreciate.

I understand you have been so conditioned to feel guilt that it is very foreign for you **not** to feel guilt. Forgiveness is how to let go of guilt. But, how do you forgive yourself when you do not feel worthy of forgiveness? The best way you can accomplish this is to give your inability to forgive to God, your Creator. You created your guilt, so realize that you cannot know how to forgive it. It is beyond your capacity to forgive yourself without the help of your Creator.

You need to fully give your desire for forgiveness to God. Ask God to do it for you. You have to do this consciously. You have to accept that you have this lack of self-forgiveness in the first place and then you need to have a true desire to let go of it. I help people get to this point. My purpose, as the angel I am, brings people freedom from anger toward others, to awareness of their guilt, to freedom from guilt, and to freedom from the inability to achieve self-forgiveness. My work is very rewarding. I have a few helper angels that assist my assigned human friends get through this time. Most of them need the help of a few different angels during this time of tremendous transformation toward self-love.

The last thing I would like to share with you is that if you help other people forgive their guilt and shame, you will likely not need my help. If you need my help to become aware of and heal your guilt, you are going to experience a very challenging wake up call. Know that this is not necessary. Helping others heal their guilt will prevent you from needing to endure this longer, more painful route.

"An angel who specializes in helping angry people"

Message from Heaven #176

I am an angel of protection. I am a powerful protector. I help people get out of a dire situation that involves a harmful or life threatening experience. People who I am given to help are stuck in a pattern of self-sabotaging behavior. Most of them have been through quite a traumatic experience in their past. As a result they have a deeply imbedded belief that they deserve to be punished. They do not consciously recognize this. They are also consciously unaware that they want to be hurt in some way. In their perception, it is a distorted way of being given attention, which makes them feel important. It actually makes them feel like they are the center of attention.

If you have not had a similar traumatic past experience you may not understand this type of behavior. It is a result of being abused. They connect the act of being given attention, as being loved. They mistakenly feel more loved when they are being abused. If someone were not giving them this type of behavior and attention, they would be left alone and feel more unloved. It is this distorted perception that creates such life-threatening experiences for them. They are seeking love so desperately and this is the only way they know how to feel important enough to be given attention – even though it is abusive, harmful attention.

The people I am given to help also have been given several other angels to help them heal their perception. They have very broken hearts. Jesus wants them to heal and grow beyond these past painful experiences, to gain freedom from them. Other angels are helping these people in very specific ways they need at that time. I am only with them when they need my immediate help to get through a life threatening situation they created. My angel friends call me when I am needed. I then come help my human friend and then I leave.

I have the ability to influence very sick minded people who are filled with angry, aggressive energy. I do nothing with the human who is in the life-threatening situation. I go to work with their aggressor. I am able to get into their hearts, you could say, and bring them back to a memory of a time they were abused by someone they loved.

I slow down events for this person, I alter the energy in their body just long enough for them to feel the feelings they felt during that experience. It is a specific way of manipulating energy that allows their suppressed pain to arise, be remembered and felt. This creates a change of heart; an immediate change of heart. Loving and compassionate energy rushes out of their heart and they are changed forever. They do not want to continue being angry or aggressive anymore. This changes this situation immediately and for the rest of their lives.

I do help the person who was going to be harmed, but I directly help the person who is about to do the harmful action. I unblock a deeply buried pain from their past and a surge of loving energy flows through their heart as a result.

I am speaking to you now to tell all of you humans who read this that these abused people need your help. Both of these types of abused people need your loving, caring help. You are intended to help your human friends heal their broken hearts. Know that your heart will be healed by helping them heal theirs. Angels are actually not intended to be needed to help humans. But, humans have so lost their natural way of living that you presently need an insurmountable number of angels just to help you get through your lives.

If more of you lived your lives to help other people heal and grow, you also would heal and grow and in time, you would not need the help of angels anymore. You would all be in love with yourselves, your lives and with each other. It is not natural for you to need our help.

I am asking you to seek to help these injured souls; these broken souls. You do not understand how easy it is to correct your world's ills. Spend some time each day giving your love and care to someone who needs help; someone you do not know. Help not only your family and friends, but help others also. This will heal your world.

"An angel of protection"

Message from Heaven #177

I am an angel in heaven. I help the souls of people who pass on. The reason I am talking to you is because these human souls, who one day will also include you, need to understand something very important.

Should you die while fearing your death because you feel unworthy of uniting with God, you will not fully transition to your true state of awareness, which is heaven. You will be held back, so to speak, from unifying with God and the souls of your loved ones.

I help these people. Basically, I try to get their attention. I am so beautiful and so loving. The light I emanate is an incredibly powerful energy that draws people's souls to me. If they are willing to look above, to me, that is all I need to influence them enough to follow me. I take them to heaven.

But, if they have a heavy amount of guilt when they die, this prevents them from be willing to look at the light I shine. They literally stay looking down at earth and they will not look up at me. I need only a split second of them looking up at me to get the opportunity to take them to heaven. It is such an incredibly beautiful experience for me to take souls to heaven. I am very grateful to be able to help people in this way.

But, too often, I am not able to help them. They feel strong fear about joining God. This is because they feel much guilt. They simply do not feel worthy of God's love. So much so, that they fear God. They think God will be angry or disappointed with them for what they've done or didn't do, and who they chose to be in their life. They are afraid to see God.

Most of these people were taught to fear God at a very young age. They grew up being told they were "sinners", or in some way, bad people. They grew up feeling a lot of guilt for not being more perfect. They believe their very nature is bad. That being said, at the core of everyone's heart is unconditional love. Unconditional love is underneath all of their developed fears. They may have been taught this too, but these are very contradicting teachings. So, they developed the fear of themselves as being not good enough for God.

One's consciousness does not change just because their soul left their physical body. One's consciousness remains the same as it was when they died. Humans have to develop their consciousness. This evolution must occur during their experiential lifetime and it does not happen without their allowance. They have to be willing to let go of all of their fear to develop a fully unconditional loving consciousness. This is usually a very slow process for humans. I'd like to help you learn how to heal your guilt. If you are one who fears God, this will save you from missing out on the most incredible experience imaginable – our home – heaven.

When you help others heal their guilt and fears, at the same time you automatically and effortlessly heal yours as well. It is so simple. Many of you only help those people who you already know and care about. That is helpful too. But, when you help someone you don't already personally know, it is a selfless action. Performing selfless actions are an extremely effective way to receive back exactly what you have given them.

I understand that your world has lost much of this meaning. Selfless acts of loving, caring and giving is not practical in the eyes of many people now. You are often too busy, too stressed and too tired to give to others for nothing given in return. Many of you do not understand how this helps you much more than them.

If you could think of someone to help who particularly needs it, perhaps someone that is very broken from all the guilt and fear they carry, you would begin to experience the freedom from the guilt and fear that you carry. This will not only help you reach heaven in the spirit world, it will help you find heaven in the physical world.
"An angel in heaven"

Message from Heaven #178
I am an angel of honesty. I help people become more honest. I am given people who are unconsciously stuck in a pattern of dishonest behavior. There are basically two kinds of dishonesty. One form of dishonesty is intentional and the other form is unintentional. I help people who have become so dishonest, they do not even realize they are being dishonest. They are very unconscious.

I'd like to explain what being unconscious means. Being unconscious means you have lost awareness of truth. When I say truth, I am referring to what comes from love. Love has many different qualities. Honesty is one quality that comes from love. When someone is filled with love, they automatically become honest people. They go hand and hand. When someone lacks love, they automatically become dishonest people. When I say filled with love, I mean they feel more love toward others and themselves. Dishonesty is a quality that comes from fear. People with more fear are more dishonest.

Fear distorts your thinking, feelings and behavior. Fear creates disharmony and dysfunction. It affects every thought, every feeling and every action. It creates chaos, drama and problems. It is the cause of all chaos, drama and problems in your world.

Self-deceit is one method of coping with the presence of fear. People who are dishonest with themselves often are not consciously aware of it. These are the people I help. I bring them more awareness of truth. I bring them experiences that open them to perceive differently. The experiences I help arrange for them are unpleasant for the most part. This is because such people do not want to perceive differently. They would rather hide from the truth and continue to live in their delusional, dishonest perception. This is because if they faced a more truthful perception, they would have to face their fear of feeling guilt. They would come to realize they have an enormous amount of guilt. They much prefer to continue to avoid acknowledging and feeling their guilt. Avoidance behavior like this creates more and more dysfunction in one's life in various ways. When someone has gotten to the point where they are near to having the willingness to face their truth, I come into their lives.

I am a master at coordinating events that will bring one to facing their truth – what they have been avoiding for a long time – their guilt. I masterfully coordinate certain situations in these people's lives that will help them see the light; the truth.

I could give you all sorts of examples of how people unknowingly lie to themselves and other people to avoid facing and feeling their guilt. But, I would rather cut to the chase and tell you that you can perceive without guilt. You can realize more truth without feeling the guilt that usually accompanies this increased awareness. You can perceive yourself differently. The pain and agony that people endure when they realize they have been living in their self-created lies, and for a long time, is completely unnecessary. I want to help you perceive this differently. I would like to help you perceive yourself the way Jesus does. Do know that He perceives everything with complete and total truth.

Jesus does not judge you for having lost the awareness of the love that you are. He does not judge you for the dysfunctional thinking and behaviors you have adopted as a result. He does not judge you for contributing to the suffering in the world. He understands that you have lost your way and don't know how to find your true-selves again. He understands that you are coping with your own dysfunction and the world's dysfunction in the best way you know how. Jesus never blames people for losing their awareness of God. He fully understands this has occurred without your understanding.

When Jesus said, "Father, forgive them for they know not what they do", He said that to make a lasting impression for all of you. He wanted you to know you are all worthy of forgiveness because you know not what you do. You have lost the awareness of your true-selves. This distorts your perception and behavior. Dishonesty is one form of dysfunction that occurs when you have lost awareness of what you really are – a fully loving being who contains no fear. Forgive yourselves. Guilt is of your own making. You have to be willing to let it go in order to be free from it. Only you can create the willingness. God cannot take it from you if you want to believe in it; if you want to hang onto it.

You are all learning how to love yourselves and others more fully. You are all learning how to be your true-selves again. Acknowledge there are many different ways you may express dishonesty. Celebrate each time you realize this. Have a party and celebrate with your friends and family when you have realized another way you have been dishonest. This means you are growing and learning and becoming more real. Do not think you should feel shame. Encourage yourself to feel happy about this progress you have made. Support each other. Encourage each other. Love each other. You are all brothers and sisters and the children of our Creator. Let go of your guilt. Do not believe you deserve such punishment.

"An angel of honesty"

Message from Heaven #179

I am an angel of peace and serenity. I bring people more peace. Peace is a quality that comes from love. I instill my loving, peaceful energy to those I am assigned to help. This energy I emanate from my being affects their energy. I simply help them feel more of my peaceful, calming energy. The people I help have very little inner peace and because of this, they are miserable. They have so much accumulated fear.

I want to help you understand that if you put your direct attention on what you fear and allow yourself to feel that which you fear and do your best not to judge yourself for having these fears, you will heal and remove more and more fear energy. It is that fear energy that literally becomes stored inside your physical cells.

The people I am assigned to help have had so much fear energy stored within their bodies for so long, they have developed a physical health problem. They are usually very sick by the time I come to them. They need my help very much. They need more peaceful energy. My peaceful energy tames their disorderly energy. I just give them my loving and peaceful energy. I love these people very much. I smile at them with love constantly. In time, they start to feel it – more peace and serenity. This is all I do.

After a little while, their increased peaceful energy is able to attract a person into their life who then takes my place. At that point I leave and go help someone else again in the same way. This is my purpose. I love what I do. I give people hope. I help them feel better. And I enable them to attract someone who will give them a more loving and peaceful experience.

If they are able to accept love from that person, they will usually get better and heal. If they struggle to accept that person's love and care, they will likely not get better, and will become increasingly sick until they die. Either way, I helped them feel more loving, peaceful energy for a time. I feel so grateful to do this for others. I help them feel the peace of God as we do. It is a gift to share this quality from love. I shine with joy when I help others know how it feels to have more peace. It is such a beautiful feeling.

Question: How do you angels get assigned your "jobs"?
Angel: Jesus always assigns us those who are in need of our help. It is always Jesus that directs us.

Question: Archangels don't sometimes tell you who to help?
Angel: No. Archangels help countless people with their area of expertise at the same time. An angel like me always helps one person at a time. Archangels are able to help many, many people at the same time.

Question: Does Jesus assign them their work also?
Angel: Yes.

Question: Can people get an angel assigned to them by asking for one? Or, do they **not** need to ask for their help because they come automatically when they need them?
Angel: We come when Jesus asks us to come to you. When you ask for an angel to come help you, then Jesus will always bring you an angel. It is very, very helpful to ask for our help. You will receive much more help from many more angels when you ask for it. We want you to ask for our help so very much. We are able to do more when you ask us for our assistance. We are happy and delighted when you ask us to help you. The more that people ask for us, the more opportunities we have to spread our loving qualities. We are here to help you.

Question: Can we pray for an angel's help for someone else? Does that help others receive the help of an angel?
Angel: Sometimes, yes, sometimes, no. That person has to also be willing to want our help.

Question: Can you tell me the difference between an angel and a spirit guide?
Angel: An angel is a spiritual being and has always been a spiritual being. Our form is an energy that is a less dense than yours. It is a non-physical energy.

Also, we are fully-loving beings and have always been fully-loving beings. We have never experienced fear.

What you call spirit guides were once humans. They are now in their spirit form and have been assigned to 'follow' another human during their life. Spirit guides are presently learning and evolving through the human's life experiences. Spirit guides are not yet fully-loving beings. They are still evolving. This does not mean they are not very loving; just not fully loving yet. Although, there are also some spirit guides who have not developed much love at all yet. They are at various stages in the development of their loving consciousness. They are not usually able to influence the human they are with like angels can.

Humans are given choice. They have the ability to choose the type of being they wish to be. They can choose between love and fear. We angels do not have the ability to experience fear.

Question: Do you know why we humans were given the choice to love or fear? That seems unfair to me because we come into the world that way. This makes me feel like a victim.

Angel: There is a most profound blessing that comes with having that choice. It is a true gift. I understand why you feel as you do right now. But, in time, you will come to realize the true gift it is. You, human souls, wanted to be your own creators. Simply put, you wanted to have the ability to create whatever you wanted to create. You wanted to have the experience of learning the difference between love and fear, that is, the difference between unity and separation. Learning this is a process which develops much love and gratitude; far more than we angels are capable of experiencing. You wanted the experience of becoming one again. If you are already one, you cannot experience becoming one. It is a most beautiful process to experience more and more of the love that you are.

Question: It does not sound like you angels have any shortage of feeling love and gratitude. You sound like you are filled with love, joy, peace and

gratitude. Your answer is not very satisfying to me. Why would anyone want to experience the pain of fear and separation?
Angel: To become God again. The experience of becoming God again is the highest experience of love one can experience.

Question: One of you angels just recently said you "were God in a non-physical form, as we humans are God in a physical form". So, you already have the realization that you are God. For a human, isn't that the goal?
Angel: We do already realize we are God, yes. But, the **experience of realizing** you are God is like no other. It is challenging for you to understand the gift that is in this until you start experiencing more God, which is pure love energy. When you start experiencing more Love Energy, you will start to understand the gift in the experience of developing it.

Comment: I'm still not quite satisfied with that answer, but I guess I will have to accept that I cannot fully understand this yet.
Angel: I will give you an example that may help you better understand the beautiful blessing of this experience. Imagine a husband and wife who are together and are both very much in love and very happy. Now, imagine their time meeting each other; spending time together; learning about themselves and each other together; growing their love together. Imagine their "once in a lifetime" experiences of falling in love with each other. This is how it is for humans. They get to experience falling in love with God. All of you humans wanted to experience the most beautiful process of realizing you are God again.
"An angel of peace and serenity"

Message from Heaven #180
I am an angel of joy. Happiness and joy is a quality that comes from love. I specialize in helping people become filled with more joy. I am filled with joy. I have fun helping people have fun. I love helping people remember what it is like to feel like a child again – filled with love and joy.

A heavy heart, a serious mind-set, a judgmental attitude, an angry person, a depressed person…these are the types of people I am assigned to help; people who have developed one or more of these outlooks. They are simply very unhappy. They have lost the ability to feel joy. They have a heavy heart.

I come to people who particularly need to feel joy. This is what they need most when I am assigned to help them. I help them feel like a child again. I help them have fun with their life. I instill a lightheartedness quality in them. Happy-go-lucky is me. I am filled with happiness and joy.

I know how to have fun in nearly any situation. I know how to make life a lot more fun. I have a great sense of humor. I can laugh and giggle about almost anything. I love being who I am. I am very playful. Silly is me. Everyone loves my influence, too, because I help them have more fun. I bring people more light, laugher and joy. I give people a spark of these feelings. They start to lighten up soon after I am with them. Their very serious attitudes begin to lighten. I bring them smiles. They actually start smiling more soon after I am with them. I get very excited about this. I love sharing my joy with them. I love helping them remember what it's like to feel like a child again – light-hearted and filled with joy.
"An angel of joy"

Message from Heaven #181

I am an angel of humility. I help people become open to receiving the grace of God. Humility is often misunderstood. When one has developed humility, their heart is more open. An open heart is needed to allow more love to flow through it. Humility is a beautiful feeling that comes from love. Increasing your humility creates more loving experiences in your life. The more humility you develop, the more you are open to receiving loving experiences. Why, you might ask? Because your heart becomes more open, less guarded, less judgmental and less fearful.

A quality of willingness accompanies the quality of humility. It is the willingness to be less evil. By "evil", I mean less fearful and less separating in your perception and behavior. People with more humility also have more inner peace. It goes hand and hand.

Many people think that humility makes them vulnerable, weak or guilty. This is an incorrect belief. It is another form of self-deceit which is used to avoid facing your fear of not being good enough. When I am assigned to help a human develop more humility, it is because they are hiding this truth. They have a deep wound in their heart. And, they cover up the wound by developing a distorted perception that they are, in some way, superior to someone else or superior to a situation they are experiencing.

Sometimes they are aware of this self-created superiority and sometimes they do not know they have this perception. Some were raised to think that way and do not know any other way. It is a deeply rooted distorted perception.

These are the people I help. I bring these people to their knees, so to speak. I bring them an experience that will humble them. If they are willing to not resist this change of events in their life, then I leave them, as they do not need my help anymore. If they resist this experience with anger, resentment or bitterness, I stay with them and bring them another experience that will humble them some more. Eventually, when they are able to perceive in a more truthful way, a more loving way, they do not need me anymore.

A different angel then comes to them and helps them develop more self-forgiveness. I love helping people in this way. I help people let go of beliefs that are not in alignment with love; that which inhibits their ability to love others and themselves more. After I am with them, they are able to love more. I know what is around the corner for them when I leave them – the experience of giving and receiving more love.

Grace then enters their life like never before. Grace means less resistance energy within you and this creates a magical experience. One becomes more open to God then, whether they consciously know it or not. An easier life with fewer obstacles begins to occur for them. Many circumstances that were troubling before automatically fade away and a beauty enters their life; ease and grace. The heart opening more with love brings grace into their direct experience.

"An angel of humility"

Message from Heaven #182

I am an angel that brings people fulfillment; a fulfillment like no other. This is my area of expertise. I am a very happy angel and I love what I do to help people become free. Freedom from a big fear comes when I am assigned a human to help. They are near ready to let go of a fear that has greatly limited their life experience their whole lives. It is always a big fear I help one become free of.

I would like to help you understand how to overcome your biggest fears. What I am referring to is healing them. So many people experience the same hurts and disappointments throughout their lives, again and again and again. Such experiences may involve different people and somewhat different situations, but always it is a similar occurrence that causes the same painful emotions.

As a result, these people eventually tend to get wrapped up in deep anger or self-pity. Engulfed in self, they become self-destructive in one way or another and rarely do they get out of this dark pit of mental anguish. All joy becomes lost and a cloud of darkness envelopes their physical experiences.

This heartbreak and lost joy for life is all because they keep running and hiding from their fears. If they would simply face them and allow themselves to feel the fearful experience in their mind and heart, without actually having to experience it, they would soon become free; free of their biggest fears.

Healing your fears truly can be this easy. When you face them and feel them, even though only in your imagination, you will come to accept them and the power from those fears will just fade away. These fears will become meaningless to you. You will come to a place where your fear no longer has control over you. Peace replaces the resistance to your fears through the acceptance of them.

Fulfillment energy then comes into your mind, heart and body. Your consciousness is greatly raised. This simply means you have allowed more Love Energy to expand from within. It is your Love Energy that is your home. When it flows through you more, with less restriction, a fulfillment like no other enters your awareness.

This is the experience I bring to humans. I give them the needed strength and courage to face their fears. And, after they do, I go help someone else. It is a high purpose of mine to help people get through a big fear. But I do wish I were not needed. You can save yourselves from much unnecessary pain. Sit back, relax and face and feel your fears – one by one - until the fear power is gone. This will prevent you from needing to create (attract) actual fearful experiences to accomplish this healing.

I hope my insight can help you understand how futile it is to resist facing your fears.

"An angel of fulfillment"

Spiritual Priorities

Message from Heaven #183

My present goal for humanity is to have more people desirous of making their spiritual growth a priority in their life. Some people do this already, but their immediate surroundings consistently inhibit them from making more significant progress. So many cities have people caught up in a busy, stressful and unnatural way of living. They emit stressful energy in their immediate surroundings and it adversely affects others in the vicinity. This suppresses their ability to expand their spirit.

I would like to explain more about what spiritual growth means in a simplistic manner. To expand your soul means that you allow it to expand. Expanding your soul means you are allowing your Source of loving, peaceful life energy to grow within your physical body and consciousness. This makes you think, feel and behave more in alignment with love. Love Energy creates the qualities and experiences that come from God, which is pure Love Energy.

The more your soul expands, the more loving, peaceful, happy, joyful, trusting, compassionate and grateful you feel. Fulfillment becomes you. It is that fulfillment which comes from unifying with God, your Source of love energy. When you are growing your spirit, you are healing your fear and growing your love. Fulfillment occurs naturally. It is the fulfillment you are all seeking, yet cannot find from the physical world.

Most of you have absorbed stressful energy and continue to accumulate more and more within your body's cells and consciousness. But if the presence of those who are in close proximity were to unite together in unison and harmony, you would all gain an increase of shared power to overcome the suppressing influences of stress. Your cooperative presence together would create a supportive influence in the consciousness for everyone.

I'd like to explain more about how to create neighborhoods or small villages just like other neighborhoods throughout your country (and others), but which would also support each other to grow spiritually; a neighborhood where the residents are interested in the growth of their soul more than the growth of their ego.

This simply means that their primary desire is to spiritually evolve; that they are willing to spend some time everyday enabling their soul to grow. This can mean they meditate daily, allowing for a time of stillness which more deeply enables their source of loving, peaceful energy to expand from within; to intentionally heal their accumulated pain and fear - the accumulated stress energy from their past experiences. Connecting with others regularly to share your knowledge, thoughts, experiences and teachings that focus on a loving, uniting energy, would greatly uplift the consciousness of the entire community and affect the rest of the surrounding world as well. Simply put, you help each other learn, heal and grow spiritually.

Individuals, families and groups in such a community could exist interdependently in a healthy, peaceful and balanced way. This would mean each neighborhood could be structured in a self-sustaining way. This does not mean to be intentionally isolated from the rest of the world. Rather, to have the capacity to live well independently without the sole reliance of outside resources, especially during times of emergency.

This includes food, shelter, clothing, water, power, medical care, education, protection for the community, etc. This could also include the residents contributing their natural passions and talents, making it easier for everyone to fall in love with their lives.

The world has lost the ability to live naturally in accordance with their soul's desires. This simply means to be in love with your lives, yourselves and each other. Some of you may wish to simplify your lives to enable this different lifestyle for you and your family. What is your purpose in this life? It is to be in love with your life, to spend your time doing that which you love doing and continuing to unify with love while expressing and sharing it with others.

Many of you have lost your way. Too many lives have little meaning, little joy and little peace. Sickness, famine and suffering run rampant in your world. This is because most of you are not living your lives in accordance with the divine – in a loving, peaceful, happy way.

So many have become like robots, living to serve yourselves, your country and your societies and your communities in a way of unbalanced, unhealthy and unhappy living. Too many people have conformed to a destructive, loveless, non-connecting way of life.

Many of you do not even realize how you have become 'enslaved' or dependent on others who are not looking out for your best interests and who are supporting the destruction of your own world. You do not question how your world has become this way. It is 'normal' to many of you.

When you come to face the truth of what you are avoiding – that you are continuing to support the ongoing deterioration of your own lives, your families, your fellow-man, animals and your earth, you will realize that my suggestion to create self-sustaining, happy, healthy, life-supportive and love-supportive communities, is the only way you can become free from conforming more and more to a self-destructive and life-less existence; one that continues to create more chaos, sickness, violence and despair. How imbalanced and stressful does life on earth need to become before you will want to change the trend you are on?
Jesus

Message from Heaven #184
Live to be happy. I'd like to talk about a new way of living. I'd like to give some simple suggestions for how to be healthier and happier. If your life is too busy and too stressful you will need to be open-minded to making changes; changes that you want, but in the beginning, making them will likely require some initiative.

Why will making changes that you want likely require open-mindedness and initiative? It is because your ego does not like you to be happy. And why does your ego not like you being happy? Because the ego thrives on dissatisfaction, pain and fear. The happier you become, the closer the ego is to death. So, from the beginning: The only way to increase true happiness is by connecting to me – Love, compassion and non-judgment. Increasing your love, compassion and non-judgment is the only way. If your happiness is reliant on anything, anyone or any circumstance, you will eventually come to realize that him, her or it, did not and cannot make you happy after all.

A lot of you already do understand this, yet you continue on with the same pattern of forgetting it. You continue living the same way - a way that does not create happiness. Pain and suffering is not happiness. Mediocrity is not happiness. So, this includes many of you. I will keep it simple. You must spend some time every day intentionally evolving spiritually; intentionally expanding your spirit. Your spirit is the "Life" of love energy and many of you have significantly lost touch with this a long time ago.

Some of you know these suggestions I am about to mention, believe they will work, but will still not do them. This is because your ego does not want you to be happy. So, for your sake and for the sake of others, begin a new way of living; one where you do not allow the ego to limit your happiness anymore. Live to be happy.

- Acknowledge, feel and heal your suppressed pain. Do the *HOPE Technique* daily.
- Meditate daily. The effect of this time spent in stillness is accumulative.
- Every day, plan a specific way to help someone feel more loved.
- Eat three meals a day alone in silence or with enjoyable company.
- Help a child or animal have fun every week.
- Form or join a group with whom you feel you are in alignment. Meet regularly with this group to discuss the personal and spiritual growth of everyone; the good, bad and the ugly. Perhaps you could meet together weekly to discuss your personal experiences of applying each of these suggestions. You will help each other learn, heal and grow by sharing your experiences.
- Examine what you think are your past errors and faults; write them down. Accept them. If you do not feel a genuine rightness in accepting them, do something about it. If you cannot bring yourself to accept them, help others who have 'faulted' in a similar way.

- Be loving and kind to others no matter what.
- Communicate your true feelings with others. Be honest while also being kind.
- Surrender everything you need help with to God; a need, a desire, a fear, a problem.
- Thank God every day for at least ten things for which you are grateful.
- Make amends with your past. Make the past right. Apologize for any wrong doings from the past to make the situation 'right' if you can. If you cannot, choose to do some good to a person or an animal for a time. Improve their life. Choose someone other than a family member or friend.
- Be able to do what you love and do it often if it is good for you.
- Write down your fears. Ask yourself why you think you have them. Acknowledge why you have them. Then surrender them to God. Ask God to free you from them.
- Ask God every day to free you from the limitation of ego (self).

If you follow these simple suggestions for creating a new life, you will expand your spirit – your love energy. Your happiness will increase quickly and you will become very powerful. By this I mean, full of the power to create more good in your life - much more good.
Jesus

Message from Heaven #185

A new life on earth is my goal for humanity; the creation of a different way of living; a daily life that is conducive for developing God awareness. This is achievable. You must want this enough to become it. Know that you are not waiting on me for the development of God Consciousness. I am waiting on your willingness to desire it enough to receive it.

You can say you want God awareness, but if you do not develop God awareness, you will not achieve it. Do you know why you are missing the awareness of who you really are? Think about this for a minute. Why do you not experience fullness of life? What is the underlying, insecure feeling that is always there? Why do you feel something is missing? Why do you experience a limited life? Why do you ever feel less than totally in love with your life? Is it because that is 'normal'? That life is just that way? What is blocking you from realizing you are all One?

All of you are the One experiencing through a different form simultaneously. You are the One already, but you have forgotten this. To be this is to know this. To awaken and expand your awareness to know this, you need to live your lives differently.

Many of you think that to receive God Consciousness, you must first sacrifice fun, joy, doing what you love doing and even your very life. Obtaining my level of awareness creates doing what you love doing - more than you could imagine - more joy, more fun, and with more Life energy.

Let go of the stories you have heard that are not in alignment with truth. I am not angry nor condemning nor boring. My life on earth was to bring you more Life; more of our Father's life. Do not believe that a sacrificing life accompanies me. It is the extreme opposite.

What you are all wanting is for your body to fully illuminate your Source of Love Energy. There is no sacrifice needed to experience fullness of life. Every day lived without awareness of God is a sacrifice you do not understand. Bring forth your willingness to grow. Know you will lose nothing but fear.

Jesus

Message from Heaven #186

When you become open enough to receive more love from your Source of Love, the most beautiful feeling starts to become you; peace, surrender, love and a gratitude to who or what is creating this feeling. It starts to come alive from inside. It is a completely new and unfamiliar feeling you have never experienced before. It does not come from the physical world and you know this.

The initial awakening of God's love is born within your body; your heart. A letting go of the past has occurred to enable this flow of Love Energy. Tuning into this feeling becomes wanted by you more and more. You will naturally desire more time in stillness to get further acquainted with this Life Energy. A personal relationship with your Source of Love is now awakening within your awareness.

This is the most precious and beautiful time imaginable. Your innocence is returning. Separation is dissolving. The experience of oneness begins to be known. Fear starts to detach from you spontaneously. An effortlessness enters your direct experience as you start to become the real you for the first time in a physical form.

The intimacy of this awakening of your true self is a love and beauty that cannot be described. You start to know who you really are and the magnificence of your innocence returning overshadows absolutely everything you have ever felt was important. You soon let go of any trying to control or create anything. That natural human desire becomes surrendered. You simply let go of all tendency to control your life and world. You become aware of our Father's love for you personally for the first time. My heart expands with you. Unification begins again.

Jesus

Message from Heaven #187

A global awakening is occurring now. It is a time for the collective consciousness of all on earth to choose a deeper experience of spiritually progressing or digressing. Stagnation is not being supported anymore. Our Father wants you to awaken and to know Him. He wants you all to grow into wanting Him. He wants you to grow beyond believing in His existence, into the direct experience of knowing Him. It is time to transition from a separate you to a united you; the knowing you are all One and not separate after all. This is strictly a matter of your level of awareness; your consciousness.

Most of you on earth have been at a very limited level of consciousness, stuck in the belief that you are all separate from each other and Me, your Creator. This means you are stuck in the creation of pain, separation and fear. Your thoughts, feelings and behaviors are all driven by the belief that you are a separate being, living your lives to serve yourselves.

I am not going to allow the furthering of this progression to continue much longer. By this I mean, a further, more intense decline in human behavior that supports stagnation in the development of human consciousness.

A time is near when you will all be given a choice to make; not one by default, but a conscious choice. On earth, there is a fork in the road to which you are all growing near. This time has been discussed by many spiritual teachers of many cultures, modern scientists and physicists, other spirit communicators like Connie, the few remaining primitive communities and from those who partook in the writings of the Bible and other Holy books from various cultures.

Stagnation will not be supported anymore. Now is the time to grow. It is no mistake your world is becoming more controlled by a government body toward conforming to a more enslaved way of living. By this, I mean when a government body becomes more controlling of the quality of your personal lives. This includes limiting your freedoms to make personal decisions for yourselves on how you want to live your lives.

How and what you eat is no longer going to be an option made by you. How you choose to heal your body of health issues is no longer going to be your choice. Poisoning or not poisoning your body is no longer going to be a choice made by you. The faiths and belief systems you choose for yourselves are no longer going to be elective. It will be decided for you by governmental bodies, which will be controlled by a one-world governmental body. The information and education choices available for you and your children will be controlled. Other freedoms will be taken away from you. The location you live in will no longer be a choice made by you.

The ability to be materially abundant will be limited to the very few. A healthy and balanced way of living will be available to the very few. An industrial way of living is in the process of being created for the majority of you. The quality of your life will be much suppressed. Complete and total dependence on a world government is being formed and will dominate the majority of you. Only two percent of you will not be included in this conformed, suppressed, limited way of living.

If you are not presently connected to this already existing world government, you are not among the two percent. All religions will be annihilated.

None will be permitted to be followed or honored publically. This world government will take away all religion's ability to influence the world. They will be suppressed into omission. The tables are being turned in these ways already. Violence, chaos and disorderliness are being induced intentionally to support the need for dependency on a military force for order and protection and further rules and regulations. A weaker citizenship of less individuality in all countries is being formed.

I want to tell you why this is occurring. It is because the majority of you on earth will not come together in a more loving, caring and unifying way unless there is more intense suffering for the majority. You have lost your way. Living to care for and serve your fellow brothers and sisters has been forgotten. You have become reliant on serving only yourselves and your own families, without caring enough about the suffering of your fellow brothers and sisters, the animal kingdom and the earth. More caring hearts would not accept this. You have become so engulfed in living to serve your selves, your own physical, material needs and desires, that you have lost awareness of and the connection to your heart's desires - which is for the loving kindness and goodness for all life on earth.

This lack of compassion toward others, including all beings of earth, cannot be transformed into caring action without a tremendous wake-up call. Many feel they do not directly cause this suffering and so continue their lives by ignoring the neglect and suffering of others. You have allowed this suffering to continue and this allowance has progressed to a point where it has created what is now happening. This has and will affect your personal lives and world in the ways I have just described. The majority of you will become mistreated, neglected, suppressed and suffering.

Know this is not punishment from God, but is the result of your own creation. All of you, collectively, create all the events in your own world here on earth. The significant minority of those who have been helping to enhance the collective consciousness will be receptive and guided to this knowledge from me through Connie and other sources of similar knowledge. This will position you to safe places throughout the globe in a way to further grow and create a new life on earth.

I have shared with you the knowledge, understanding and guidance needed to spiritually evolve into a unity consciousness, individually and collectively. In the near future, you will be given a choice to make by a governing body to further conform to their way of living. This means to be owned, controlled and governed by a number. Their way may seem to be an easier way of life with use of their numbers. However, know that it will mean the loss of your freedom and ability to continue growing toward God consciousness in your lifetime on earth.

Those who choose not to accept this number will need to join together in small communities and become capable of self-sufficient and self-sustaining living within each community. That means living without relying on outside sources for your survival needs. Follow my guidance and suggestions in these messages about the formation of such communities. My way of living simply means growing and expanding your love for yourselves and for all others. Know that if you are following my way of living you will have my personal support and protection.

Jesus

Your Soul's Call to Awaken

Message from Heaven #188

WHAT ARE YOUR personal goals right now? What are your heart's desires? What are you yearning for? What are you trying to create in this life? These are questions to ask yourself. I'd like to explain how to bring together your earthly human desires and your soul's desires as well.

Your human identity wants experiences from the physical world. Your soul wants the experience of reunion with your Creator. Developing God consciousness in the physical world is one of both action and non-action (stillness). How do you live in the physical world with physical needs and desires, while also honoring your soul's call to spiritually awaken?

It is intended that you grow your awareness toward God consciousness while also participating in life on earth. You are meant to experience both the inner and the outer qualities of life together.

Some spiritual seekers remove themselves from society to be alone and more reclusive to partake in spiritual practices. They can make some spiritual progress, but go from creating one imbalanced state to another imbalanced state. After a period of time, other imbalances develop as a result of not participating in the world and their spiritual growth again becomes challenging.

I want to tell you how to experience the best of both the physical and the spiritual simultaneously. This means living in the physical world while also intentionally growing spiritually toward God awareness. This is how I define balanced living. It is the integration of consciousness into *both the physical and spiritual.*

Creating a regular, balanced daily routine greatly helps. Spontaneous right action occurs as you become more in balance with right living. I'd like to offer a basic, daily schedule; one that creates living a balanced life. Balanced living allows for more rapid spiritual expansion and getting to know your Source of love - God.

I want you to know what a balanced life is like, as most of you have no idea anymore. Imbalanced living is a great impediment to growing your soul. Living your life in sync with nature, with the rhythm of life, of natural and spontaneous right action, has become devalued in your society.

For those who are ready and want to know how to live a daily life in alignment with growing your soul, here is a good general guideline: Wake up as the sun rises and go through your daily activities. Transition yourself toward a more relaxed state with the setting of the sun and go to sleep near the high rising of the moon.

1. Begin your morning connecting with your Source - the presence of God. Talk to God, connect with God consciously. Meditate. Listen to your inner intuition. This is a time for stillness; a time to develop your inner qualities that come from soul expansion.
2. Spend about six hours a day working, doing what you love. Do that which feels like your purpose. This includes following your passion. Do work that you are naturally good at, or want to be, and that is enjoyable to you. Do work that also contributes toward the good of humanity, the community in which you live and for the good of all on earth.
3. Eat meals at about the same time each day. Eat in a relaxed, non-active way.
4. Acknowledge God throughout your day. Remember He is with you. Connect with God in your mind and heart. Tell Him you want Him to grow and expand within. Tell God you love Him and want to unify with Him; that you want to be in alignment with His desires and to serve Him throughout your life on earth. Think of God throughout your day; talk to Him; share your thoughts with Him; your needs, your desires, your fears, your feelings and what you feel grateful for.
5. Allow freedom-time during your day to be spontaneous. This simply means to be able to take breaks from your work for fun, for relaxing,

for helping someone with their needs, to take a walk or other form of exercise, to spend time in nature, to have enough flexibility to do so throughout your day. Allow for time to enjoy friends and family. Be present in your awareness; avoid multi-tasking.
6. Before your evening meal, have another time in stillness for deeper connection to God. Meditate. Commune with your soul. Feel your heart's love grow for the love of God and your life. This is another time to tune into stillness.
7. Eat dinner and do not work afterward. It is a time to relax and settle down before sleeping.

This is a general structure for you to live a well-balanced life. As you begin to settle your mind's activity and your nervous system, you will begin to integrate your natural peaceful energy into your active, waking state. Your emotional state will become more in alignment with the natural state of harmony, love and joy. Spontaneous right action develops automatically. Connecting with the divine deepens and in time begins to create your life for you. You will do less to accomplish more.

This would bring a quality of ease and grace to your lives on earth. Most lives are formed in a continuous state of stress and irritation and emptiness, with little or no soul growth. This is why there are extreme imbalances at all levels on earth at this time. The only way to transition into right living, which means your natural way of living that creates a joyful, purposeful and fulfilling life, is to start living your lives in a way that allows for the further growth and development of your soul.

A life of extreme busyness has become an addiction that most people on earth have developed. This is the opposite of a life connected with God. Society is becoming more and more of a God-less existence. This creates more sickness, dysfunction and suffering for all life on earth.

Learn to become comfortable being in stillness. Become comfortable with a more relaxed, carefree and joyful life; one with connection to God's love through the connections to His life forms on earth. Remember that His love needs to be experienced more to become more of Him. This means experiencing love, fun and happy times with your family and friends, animals and earth's life forms (nature). Cultivating your love energy is cultivating the God within you.

Question: Jesus, many people would love to have the luxury of this daily routine as you describe. Most of us are not so free to live our lives this way unless we are independently wealthy. Most in my country (USA) have to work way too many hours just to meet their basic needs. Many families have both parents working and do not have time for stillness, meditating and connecting with you, nor for relaxed, fun times doing what we love. What can you suggest for the majority of us who are not independently wealthy and are unable to schedule our time as we would like to?

Jesus: First, you must want this. Many of these people you refer to do not genuinely want this. They are already addicted to a stressful, busy life without God or a deeper loving connection with others. They do not know enough to want more. They voluntarily accept living a numb and lifeless, loveless, joyless and unconscious, "busy" existence, disconnected from the presence and awareness of God.

For those who truly want a different life, I suggest you prioritize your goals, desires and time to support and enable this quality of life. Give God your desire for this. Do what you can in the meantime to go in this direction. Live simply. God **will** support this desire if it is genuine. But, you must start putting your thoughts, desires and energy into creating this first.

Jesus

Message from Heaven #189

When you care enough about developing your consciousness beyond the confines of the ego-based perception, you will begin to surrender everything you have been taught that is not in alignment with love. What you consider challenges, begin to occur more frequently. What has been giving you your sense of identity and false security begins to dissolve. One by one, the various forms of your identity become lost in one way or another; health, money, a position, a loved-one, a lifestyle, your status or reputation, possessions.

It is the losing of yourself - your ego-self - that begins to make room for your Higher-Self to awaken. What you have mistakenly learned to rely on for your false sense of peace, confidence and self-worth becomes completely lost. You are now ready to learn how to rely on me for all you need. You may not be comfortable doing this at first. This is typically a frightening process and you often resist accepting these changes. It is this resistance which causes you suffering. It also strengthens fear-based emotions; anger, guilt, jealousy, sorrow and self-pity.

During these times of unwanted loss and change, know it is an opportunity for you to develop the willingness to transition toward trusting God to take over your life. But, you would rather believe you are the one in control of your life, so you typically continue to allow your ego's-identity to strengthen. You become more and more engulfed in your resistance and fear. Suffering continues. You do not want to surrender that which you have learned is merely the idea of who you are. Many of you will resist to your very death rather than to let me guide you through what I want for you. You do not yet trust me.

You cannot learn how to trust in me until you surrender your resistance to the loss of what you are experiencing. It is important for you to consciously remind yourself that you have absolutely no control over your life. You may think that you are the one that created your life as it is, but know that you have what you have because God has given it. Consciously acknowledging this brings is a more surrendering perception. What is the value in this? You begin the process of learning acceptance. Through the acceptance of what you are resisting, comes the loving power of God into your life. The peace that passes all understanding begins to emerge from within. This has nothing to do with the circumstances in your life being in alignment with your personal desires.

This is growing up spiritually; the maturing of your soul. When you notice you want to change your present moment experience, for any reason whatsoever, remind yourself that it is God who has all the power. Doing this one, simple mental reminder will help this process of growth come much quicker and easier.

You will eventually learn how to unify with God's will. This means that you want to allow it, whether the present experience is your personal preference or not. I developed the humility needed to surrender all resistance to God's will. What is the value in this? You are becoming more of our Father. You are allowing Him to grow within you. This gives you the peace of God from Him that is not dependent on outer circumstances. This is where your power lies. It lies in the allowance of God to manifest what He wants, which will bring you to oneness in your consciousness. This is the fulfillment you seek, but do not yet know of.

You do not know this is what you are constantly seeking until you have found it. You resist what your soul is striving for. Surrender your resistance to each and every moment, through each and every loss, through each and every 'challenging' experience. My grace is waiting for you. It comes when you allow your present experience to be as it is. Your trust in me will grow. Your own plans are not going to free you from the bondage of separation and fear. My plans do. Consciously surrender your resistance as it arises - again and again and again.

Have no other goal than to succumb to my will for you. This will bring you your true heritage. This will bring you what you are wanting, but have forgotten.

Jesus

Message from Heaven #190
When you come to realize that nothing can fulfill you but the presence of our Father, you begin to let go of everything you have been clinging to for happiness. You just stop wanting anything from the physical world and your mind and heart stays on God. You want nothing else but the presence of God.

This is a time of complete and total waiting. You can do absolutely nothing but wait for God to enlighten you. You are utterly helpless. Fighting this time is futile. You are meant to be in this time of waiting. You need this time of waiting to become fully open to His coming. All desires from your mind become meaningless. Everything you thought had meaning has none. You will not be satisfied with anything but God awakening within your consciousness.

Your daily existence becomes more and more empty; more and more meaningless. Your disconnection to our Father becomes more and more felt. The pain of separation becomes more intense. Recognize the gift in this. Your lessons learned are bringing you to this moment of grace.

Surrender to this. Intentionally feel the meaninglessness of your existence without God. Let your yearning for Him be felt fully. Do not resist this discomfort. Look for it. Tap into it intentionally. Honor your soul's call to awaken. Give God your thanks for this time of deeper emptiness. Acknowledge how broken you are without His direct connection. Be with it. Surrender to it and wait for Him to awaken your heart.
Jesus

Question: How do we know we have entered into this phase of our development rather than gotten off track somehow?
Jesus: You will know. The readiness for God comes after putting your energy toward achieving God awareness in a significant way.

Letting Go

Message from Heaven #191

MAKE AMENDS WITH your past. This means to let go of your past painful experiences. If you harbor and store the painful emotions (energy) from past painful experiences, you will re-create these painful experiences again and again; perhaps through a different person and a somewhat different situation. But, the past will repeat itself again and again until you have faced, felt and healed the negative energy stored within your body's cells.

Learn an effective way to face, feel and heal your accumulated pain and fear from past experiences and you will save lifetimes of unnecessary suffering. These repeated experiences are opportunities to heal this remaining energy. If you were to face what is there, you would bring freedom from your past very quickly.

I created the *HOPE Technique* for this purpose. You will not understand its full value until you have gained the benefit from doing it. Know that until you free yourself from your accumulated pain and fear energy, you will attract and create more experiences that cause the unhealed energy to surface. Skip this unnecessary and lengthy process that denies you access to your freedom. Eventually, all fear must be acknowledged, felt and honored.

Do the *HOPE Technique* daily to quickly bring yourself to freedom from your past. The *HOPE Technique* specializes in courageously facing what is not in alignment with love and annihilates it without getting involved in it. There is love and fear in the form of energy within your body's cells and consciousness. Until you heal all fear, ignorance remains and unifying with Christ consciousness is not possible.

Jesus

Message from Heaven #192

Can you see how you create one form of stressful situation after another? Can you see how you need one experience after another to feel at peace and happy? Can you see how you are continuously discontent with your present experience? Can you see how life is never good enough as it is? Do you notice you are always in a place of striving for something new, for something to be different than what it is?

This is the nature of the ego's perception; that the present is not good enough, that you are lacking something and need something more. This means you are constantly resisting the present moment as it is. This also means you are resisting God's will.

May I make a suggestion that will help you surrender this never ending path of discontentment and lack of fulfillment? Recognize that nothing in the physical world will meet your satisfaction; no person, no thing and no situation. Reaching acknowledgment of this fact creates a new beginning toward finding the peace of God that is always within you already, but unable to be felt or experienced.

This is a new beginning in your search for God. Disappointment will find you again and again, until you let go of your search for something or someone in the physical world to fulfill you. I wait for this time of realization from you.

This is when you can begin making true progress merging toward my level of awareness. This means unifying with our Father's love. Separation from our Father's love begins to melt away when you stop searching outside yourself for contentment; when you consciously acknowledge that only your Source of love can bring you fulfillment. It is a long journey in most cases to reach this time. One painful, disillusioning experience after another is this journey. I'd like to help you jump from this path to the path that leads to directly connecting with God.

God awareness is soul awareness. They are one and the same. Having the desire for soul awareness must first be present to start developing it more significantly. Your soul will not make you desire something you do not yet want. It will wait for you to desire Its growth and Its awareness. It waits for you to want to get to know It. This is when you become a "spiritual seeker". You begin to seek more than which is from the physical world.

Now, you are on the "spiritual path". A new driving force steers you in life. It is your soul expanding more, in search of Itself **through your perception**. It wants to unify with you - the human you - **through your awareness**.

It becomes a war between your ego-self and your soul-self wanting to enliven more. Your ego resists and your soul allows. Constantly, your ego wants you to feel more of it, which is dissatisfaction and fear. Your soul allows you to do what you will. For if It were to force you to It instead, It would not be out of genuine devotion for It and would not be a real expansion of more love.

It is the expansion of your love that connects you closer to your soul's awareness. Resistance energy is not loving energy. When you resist what life brings you, your soul growth is son hold. It will wait for you to be in a place of surrender to grow more. Being at war with yourself is a painful, slow process until you come to realize that you can never win.

There is no end to this insane pattern of living in ignorance. Your nature at this time is to resist whatever is. The ego's perception is resistance and the soul's perception is acceptance. Induce awareness of your soul's perception by consciously remembering to allow whatever is.

This could be the weather, your boss's feelings about you or a coworker, the driver in front of you, the conditions of your life in any area, the behavior of another person, a loved one's illness or your own, the fact that you age, your perceived limitations, whatever you feel you lack. Get to the point of recognizing that whatever is, will not be good enough.

When you can fully understand this truth, you will begin the process of learning how to surrender to what is and allow, rather than staying in the phase of resisting and trying to manipulate life to a 'better' condition, which will never suffice. Staying in this unconscious mode of resistance becomes conscious by simply recognizing your resistance. Just a simple mental acknowledgment brings awareness to it; to the unconscious pattern of your perception.

As you become more aware of how only you and your perception is what brings you all your grief, surrender can then become a part of your life. This is when you develop soul awareness. It is accomplished simply through resisting life less and less. A momentum of less resistance and more allowance enters your life and your true state of peace begins to emerge. Call it

the peace of God or the peace of your soul. It is one and the same. Resisting whatever is, is simply a habit. Bring awareness to it and you will begin your soul's journey. Fulfillment quickly follows.
Jesus

Message from Heaven #193
Take a look at your habits and you will see your pain. If your habits are less than loving to yourself or others, there is unhealed pain to face, feel and heal. Nothing will bring you true freedom from bad habits except acknowledging, facing and feeling your suppressed pain and fear.

Bad habits, such as smoking, drinking, drugging, overeating, irresponsible spending, gambling, all other addictive or compulsive behaviors, as well as less noticeable behaviors, such as telling white lies, trying to manipulate or control another's behaviors to suit your needs or desires, worry, negative thinking or criticism, are other dysfunctional behaviors that occur due to harboring suppressed unhealed pain and fear.

One can deal with the problem at the level of the problem through using your mind's will power – using mental strain and effort to control them. But, to go beyond this very limited way of healing, go straight to the root cause of these unhealthy behaviors, which is in the heart - facing the unhealed pain and fear from your past experiences.

Identify what is hiding there. You unconsciously pretend it's not there. You want to avoid it. It seems easier to ignore and keep your mind preoccupied instead. But, this is a never ending battle of the mind. Freedom will never come from adjusting your mind-set alone. This forced effort may seem to help for a time, but keeps you in the unhealed stage of coping.

Trying to correct your distorted fear-based thoughts and behaviors without also correcting the cause of them is not true healing. They are just a symptom of what needs your attention. The underlying cause of your unhealthy thoughts and behaviors is your unhealed pain. It needs your awareness, love, compassion and forgiveness.

The *Hope Technique* gets you out of your mind's thinking and connects you to the source of your diminished joy, love, peace and happiness. Put

attention on the pain that is in your heart. Get out of the story your mind has created to bypass it. Feel instead of think. No talking, no reasoning, no mental planning, no goal setting. Just feel the pain which is the underlying cause of all imbalance and un-wellness. Do this a few minutes a day using the *Hope Technique*. This gets you out of the never-ending pattern of resisting the problem, focused on trying to fix (control) the problem (the symptom). Face, honor and accept a problem to get to the cause of it. This is what brings you freedom from your ego's pain and fear and the many distortions it creates.
Jesus

Message from Heaven #194
When you make progress growing spiritually, an inner peace begins to enliven from within. It has nothing to do with the outer conditions of your life. You start to feel at home. It is an unfamiliar feeling, yet also a comforting one. You know this is what you've been missing your whole life, but were looking for it always outside yourself; from outer things, people and circumstances.

Once you start to enliven this part of your nature, there is no turning back to the darkness you now realize you've been in. You want to move forward toward further developing this inner peace. More and more you seek this newfound energy of peaceful aliveness from within. In time, you start to become it. This is when a joy awakens and it is a joy that is completely unfamiliar to you.

Your mind will start to question why and what is responsible for this joy that makes you feel more like a child again; lighter and brighter in every way imaginable. Your innocence is returning now and love infuses into your thoughts, feelings and actions like never before. A natural desire manifests to help others feel this love and joy. You are now developing a oneness consciousness. It is not something you strive for. It happens automatically.

Gratitude for life begins to blossom. This is the glory for God spoken of in the Bible. It is real. It is true. This is who you really are. It is our formless Father you have heard about. This is the beginning of the development of

Christ consciousness – my consciousness, through your mind's awareness. This is what the Bible means when it says you must go through me to find the Kingdom of God, our Father.

The truth of who you are is always within you, but cannot emerge until you are willing to let go of the darkness; the untruths your mind has chosen to believe in. They are only illusions anyway - your mind-made self, your ego-self, the devil, your fears - that were never real to begin with. Your physical form has changed many times, but only the true you is always the same; our Father's love. I want you to know this – from your heart, not your mind.

Be still and know I am God. You begin the process of knowing this when you begin to regularly still your mind's thinking. This is the only requirement for your spiritual growth to start soaring. Your pure love energy takes care of everything else spontaneously. You need not do anything more but allow it to awaken and heal what is there. **Learn how to still your mind.** Learn how to be comfortable in stillness at regular times. Otherwise, your mind will continue to take over your life and your whole world.
Jesus

Message from Heaven #195

A new purpose awaits you when your spirit-self starts to enliven; a purpose that brings the fulfillment your heart has been seeking. This purpose is for the good of all. Often, your mind does not want this purpose. It thinks it will have to sacrifice itself for it. But, the mind knows nothing of spiritual matters and cannot understand it. Know that what your mind clings to for its satisfaction and fulfillment, will never satisfy nor fulfill you. Anything from the physical world will eventually disappoint you.

When you allow your heart's desires to enter into your mind's desires, you start seeking not for self, but for others' happiness and fulfillment. Then a fulfillment, a fullness you do not yet understand, takes over. This fullness Itself is alive and starts adding to your life everything you need. You will learn how to let It take over. You will learn that It creates so much better than you do alone. You will learn to trust It. You will then be in Its' flow of creation and finally understand that what you've been doing all along was resisting It. Intentionally and voluntarily, you will then surrender to It.

Letting go of your human self is merely a transition. It is foreign at first but once you get in this flow of Life, you will never want to go back to living as before; the strain and stress of it all; a never ending battle for more. Growing spiritually is your goal. It will bring you everything you seek but do not yet know. Intellectually understanding this process helps you learn what surrender means and what it leads to. It leads to your true self awakening within your conscious awareness and becoming one with all again.
Jesus

The Collective Shift

Message from Heaven #196

MAKE A SHIFT toward the development of human consciousness world-wide. Share my messages in this book. Expand your awareness of truth; that you are here to remember who you are in a physical world and to experience your joy and share it with others.

Your world can shift dramatically from the chaos and hardship and struggle to one of harmony, love and grace. Please desire this along with me. The collective consciousness of all must be involved for I cannot do this for you.

The knowledge I've shared is all that is needed to know to create fullness of life for each of you. My suggestions are easy to apply in your life. Remember that simplicity is more successful than being complex.

I await the expansion of your desire for growth, which will bring balance and wellness and happiness to all.

Jesus

Message from Heaven #197

Initiate a regular meeting group. Come together and support each other through the practice of my suggestions. Share your own experiences. This will support your transition to conscious living.

Jesus

Message from Heaven #198

There are many of you who want to live like this, but do not believe it is practical in this modern world as it is today. But the spiritual *is* the practical. Know that it is, otherwise I would not be sharing these messages. Some of you will be in favor with them and begin to live them and look forward with joy to the forming of these new communities. I want to emphasize the importance of doing this.
Jesus

Message from Heaven #199

There is more support coming than ever before for the awakening of human consciousness. There are cycles in your bodies, in nature, in evolution. These cycles are governed by a natural force in the creation of everything. Earth is ready for a new trend. Be in alignment with it. Flow with it, not against it on your own. Know it always guides you toward your awakening to Me. It brings you balance and healing in all ways. Be open to learning more about it. Be open to trusting your own intuition. Through your soul's awareness comes everything you need to know. Try to get more in tune with it. This requires listening to it in stillness; non-activity of the mind. Practice stillness daily. You will naturally and spontaneously become more in tune with the rhythm and cycle of life that will guide you perfectly.
Jesus

Message from Heaven #200

A new life on earth is forming already. With the dissolving of one phase always comes another. Choose a higher path now and follow me, the Christ consciousness that is within you already. It is waiting only to be recognized. By expanding your consciousness you will grow toward me in your direct experience. Follow your heart and know me.

Be open to this new knowledge for it brings you closer to the birthright of your true freedom. What does this true freedom feel like? It is being totally and absolutely in love with your life. Only one thing prevents this – resisting your fear. Be courageous and face those fears to be rid of them forever. I will lead you the rest of the way for I am with you always.
Jesus

In Closing

DIVINEUNIVERSITY.ORG WEBSITE WILL soon be out of its construction phase. For this I give my gratitude to Jesus, the angels and published author of *"Divine State of Mind"*, Susan Lawrence. She is my supportive friend, gifted healer in her work as a Spiritual Hypnotherapist and truly divine business partner.

Our entire curriculum has been guided into creation by Jesus, Mahavatar Babaji and the angels. Included is the *HOPE Technique*, worksheets, detailed instructions from my books and other heavenly communications as well. These are available in text, audio and video format.

Individual courses are available. They are presented progressively in an organized, step-by-step manner making them easy to apply in your daily life. Your success is also supported interactively with other students of Divine University.

If you would like to communicate directly with spirit regarding any personal, medical or spiritual matter, I am available for private phone consultations. Visit me at: www.HelpFromHeaven.net

Connie Fox
North Palm Beach, Florida
October, 2015

www.ingramcontent.com/pod-product-compliance
Lightning Source LLC
LaVergne TN
LVHW051117080426
835510LV00018B/2083